SYLVIA PLATH

Marnie Pomeroy

GREENWICH EXCHANGE
LONDON

Greenwich Exchange, London

First published in Great Britain in 2006
Reprinted 2012

Printed and bound by imprintdigital.net
Cover design by December Publications
Tel: 028 90286559
Cover image of Sylvia Plath
courtesy of Rex Features

Greenwich Exchange Website: www.greenex.co.uk

Cataloguing in Publication Data is available
from the British Library

ISBN: 978-1-871551-88-4

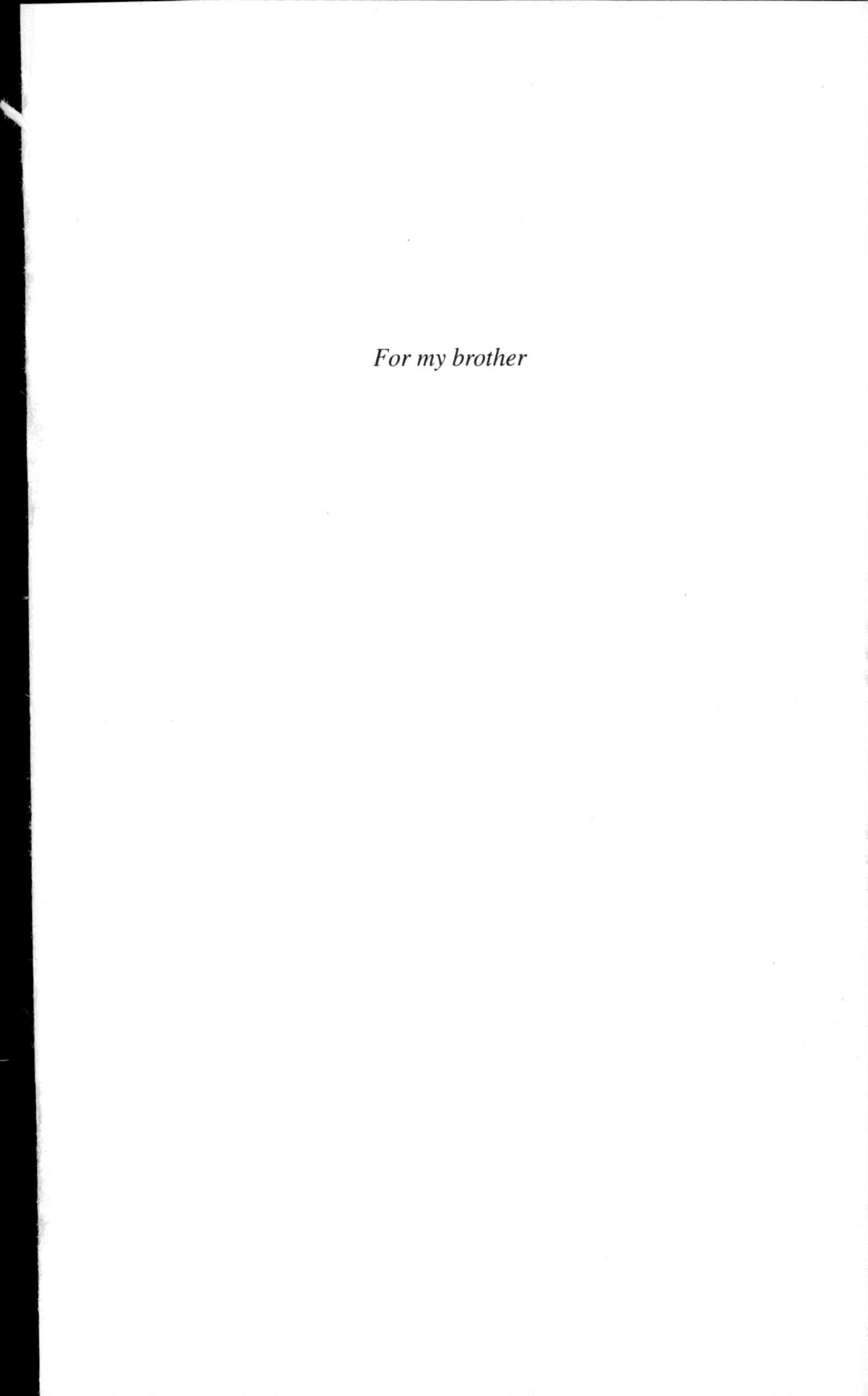

For my brother

Contents

Chronology

1932 Sylvia Plath born Thursday, 27th October, in Jamaica Plain, near Boston, Massachusetts, to Aurelia and Otto Plath.

1935 Brother, Warren Plath, born. Otto shows signs of illness.

1937 Plath family moves to Winthrop, Mass. Sylvia begins school. Saves first carefully worked poem.

1938 March: Germany invades Austria, then Yugoslavia and Greece. Pogroms in Germany.
21st September: Devastating hurricane hits the Northeast coast of the US.

1939 Death of W.B. Yeats and Sigmund Freud.
Germany invades Poland.
Britain and France declare war on Germany.
USSR invades Finland.

1940 Churchill becomes Prime Minister of Britain. Five-year Blitz on London begins.
Plath is regularly writing poems, some dated and saved.
Otto's diabetes diagnosed. A stubbed toe leads to gangrene, his leg is amputated, and a blood-clot causes his death.

1941 Deaths of James Joyce and Virginia Woolf.
The Schobers, Aurelia's parents, move in so she can return to teaching.
11th August: Plath's first poem published in the *Boston Herald*.

	7th December: Japanese bomb Pearl Harbour. President Roosevelt declares war on Germany, Italy, and Japan.
1942	Millions of Jews killed in gas chambers. Gandhi arrested for demanding India's independence. Aurelia moves family to Wellesley, Mass. Teaches at Boston University.
1943	Plath begins keeping diaries and journals. Warsaw massacre. General Eisenhower commands Allies in North Africa, then Italy, which surrenders.
1944	6th June: D-Day – the Allies, under Eisenhower, land in Normandy.
1945	President Roosevelt dies; Truman becomes President. Mussolini killed. Hitler commits suicide. 8th May: VE Day – end of war in Europe. US bombs Hiroshima and Nagasaki. 15th August: VJ Day – Japan surrenders.
1947	Plath enters Bradford High School; Wilbury Crockett her "teacher of a lifetime".
1950	Summer: Job on vegetable farm. August: First nationwide publications of a short story and a poem. September: Enters freshman year at Smith College on a scholarship. Meets Olive Higgins Prouty, her sponsor, then friend.
1951	Dates Dick Norton, medical student. Summer: Job as nanny in Swampscott, Maine. Sophomore year at Smith. Buckley coming-out party in Sharon, Ct.
1952	Summer: Jobs as hotel waitress, then as mother's helper. August: *Mademoiselle* publishes prize-winning 'Sunday at the Mintons'. Junior year at Smith begins with a serious depression.

Approached by both Knopf and Dodd, Mead about writing a novel. Breaks leg skiing while visiting Dick who is in a sanatorium with tuberculosis.
Dylan Thomas' *Collected Poems* published.
Eisenhower resigns as Supreme Commander of Europe and is elected President of US.

1953 End of term: Dates Gordon Lameyer, among others. First in her class; is awarded two important poetry prizes.
Summer: Guest Managing Editor at *Mademoiselle* in New York City. After returning home to Wellesley, collapses from depression and receives electroshock therapy.
24th August: Attempts suicide. Is institutionalised in McLean Hospital, branch of Mass. General system. Helped by psychiatrist Dr Beuscher. Learns that depression may be inherited through Otto's family.
Stalin dies, succeeded by Malenkov. Khrushchev is advanced. Coronation of Queen Elizabeth II.

1954 Early winter: Returns to Smith College. Successes and honours follow. Trips to New York. Meets Richard Sassoon.
Summer: Attends Harvard Summer School on scholarship.
Autumn: Begins senior year. Applies for Fulbright scholarship.

1955 May: Wins Fulbright scholarship to Cambridge University.
June: Receives many prizes; graduates Summa Cum Laude.
October: Begins year at Newnham College, Cambridge.
Christmas: Paris, Nice, and Vence (Matisse Chapel) with Sassoon.

1956 25th February: Meets Ted Hughes at a party.
23rd March: Visits Hughes before vacation on the Continent.

April: Trip to Germany and Italy with Lameyer.
Back to Cambridge. Attends London reception for Bulganin and Khrushchev.
16th June: Marriage to Ted Hughes, with Aurelia present.
Summer: Honeymoon in Benidorm, Spain.
Autumn: Second Fulbright year begun in Cambridge.
Soviet troops invade Hungary.

1957 Plath ends Cambridge year with final exams.
June: Returns to US with Hughes. Vacation in Cape Cod, Mass.
Autumn: Teaches Freshman English at Smith College.
Discord in marriage. Hughes' *The Hawk in the Rain* published in England and the US.

1958 Plath suffers from writer's block, then writes eight breakthrough poems.
Completes year of teaching. Moves with Hughes to Boston. Job as receptionist in psychiatric clinic at the Mass. General Hospital. Further therapy with Dr Beuscher.
Khrushchev becomes Premier of USSR.

1959 Attends Robert Lowell's poetry workshop at Boston University. Becomes a friend of poets Robert Lowell and Anne Sexton.
6th March: Urged by Dr Beuscher, visits her father's grave for the first time.
Hughes awarded Guggenheim grant.
Summer: Trip across US.
Autumn: Stay at Yaddo, writing poetry.
December: Back to England

1960 Flat rented near Regent's Park, London.
March: Hughes' *Lupercal* published; wins the Somerset Maugham Award.
1st April: Birth of daughter, Frieda Rebecca, at home.
Early summer: Faber & Faber cocktail parties and dinner at T.S. Eliot's.

October: Plath's *The Colossus and Other Poems* published by Heinemann, favourably reviewed by A. Alvarez in *The Observer*.
John F. Kennedy elected President of the US.
Brezhnev becomes President of USSR.

1961 February – March: Miscarriage of second child and appendectomy. Receives first-reading contract from *The New Yorker*. Begins *The Bell Jar*. Hughes wins Hawthornden Prize for *Lupercal*.
June: Plath records reading of her poems for the BBC.
July: Plath wins first prize in Cheltenham Festival Poetry Competition.
August: Move to Court Green in North Tawton, Devon. London flat sublet to David and Assia Wevill.
November: Saxton Foundation grant awarded to write *The Bell Jar*, long since finished and accepted for publication by Heinemann.
Construction of Berlin wall.

1962 17th January: Birth of son, Nicholas Farrar.
May: Knopf publishes *The Colossus and Other Poems* in the US. Visit from David and Assia Wevill.
9th July: Plath is given proof of Hughes' relationship with Assia Wevill. Shortly after, she burns her second novel and Hughes' manuscripts.
October: Hughes moves out. Plath is writing another novel and the *Ariel* poems.
December: She moves with children to a flat in London.
Christmas Eve: A. Alvarez visits.

1963 January: *The Bell Jar* is published in England by William Heinemann Ltd, under the pseudonym Victoria Lucas.
7th February: She and the children invited to stay with the Beckers.
11th February: Suicide of Sylvia Plath in her flat.
Death of Robert Frost. Assassination of President Kennedy.

1965	*Ariel* published in England, collection and ordering changed by Hughes. Beginning of Sylvia Plath cult.
1966	*Ariel* published in the US.
1969	Suicide of Assia Wevill; Shura, her daughter by Ted Hughes, dies with her.
1970	Aurelia Plath tries to stop Harper & Row's publication of *The Bell Jar* (Plath did not want it published in the US on account of its unkind characterisations). Ted Hughes marries Carol Orchard.
1971	*The Bell Jar* – published in the US; on *The New York Times* bestseller list for six months. Hughes publishes Plath's poems in *Crossing the Water* and *Winter Trees*.
1977	Hughes publishes Plath's *Johnny Panic and the Bible of Dreams*.
1981	Plath's *The Collected Poems* finally published (by Faber & Faber, and Harper & Row) to great praise, but Hughes' editing is criticised.
1982	*The Collected Poems* receives the Pulitzer Prize. *The Journals of Sylvia Plath* published by the Dial Press in a limited edition. 35,000 hardcover copies of first printing sell immediately.
1984	Ted Hughes named Poet Laureate of England (declined by Philip Larkin).
1994	11th March: Death of Aurelia Plath.
1997	Hughes' *Tales of Ovid* wins Whitbread Book of the Year Award.
1998	January: Hughes publishes *Birthday Letters*, serialised in *The Times*. 28th October: Death of Ted Hughes.

2000 *The Unabridged Journals of Sylvia Plath* published by Random House.

2003 The film *Sylvia*, with Gwynneth Paltrow and Daniel Craig, plays in main cinemas, and is discussed extensively, as is Plath, on the Internet in the *Sylvia Plath Forum*.

Prologue

The popular image of Sylvia Plath is sensational: the young woman who wrote poems and committed suicide. Existing in the popular mind at all is an achievement for any poet, and the 2003 film, *Sylvia*, which billed her as legendary, proves how much she still matters. Sylvia attracted notice first as a writer and then through lurid personal events, but her poetry is the star. A beacon for the young and the young at heart, the radical openness in her poems substitutes for the open expression she could never allow her person.

Not just a good girl, she was a perfect one – sunny, loving, polite, pretty, smart, and successful – who distorted part of her nature to fit the idealised norm. She also wrote startling poetry that pushes limits. More wayward than porn, it arose uninhibited from wellsprings beyond willpower, fresh in both senses: new, and also cocky. Poetry like this amounts to something subversive, with meaning or imagery circulating under the cover of words that the reader must be willing to plumb.

Consider a harsh passage that ends 'Burning the Letters', written 13th August 1962. (Precise dates are given for the composition of about half of her poems, which is useful if they relate to an event in her life.) When her husband, Ted Hughes, had left her to be with his new lover, Assia Wevill, she made a bonfire and burned the draft of her novel about their happiness, intended as his birthday present. So that the poem would relate widely, she wrote about a woman burning old letters from her attic. As she sights a charred name that pierces her with pain, she hears dogs killing a fox in the distance and applies this to herself. The fox's blood and insides and its scream burst upon the air, turn everything red – the droplets that make up the clouds, the forest leaves, the streams, puddles, and ditches. The straightforward language says what is unacceptably in-your-face terrible: that such agony, drowning the world in red, drives home what real immortality is because it lives forever, while clouds, leaves, and water merely dissolve and pass (like us).

A highly-condensed poem, one of her shortest and strongest, and the third last that she ever wrote, is 'Contusion' from 4th February 1963, a week before her suicide. She had picked an unusual subject – that one small point can be crucial if not deadly. Imaginatively illustrating this, she build a poem both creepy and sad.

Hughes having left her, she feels like someone wounded, then drowned and left in the water a long time. A perverse beauty finishes the first stanza, with the purple of a bad bruise (the contusion) at the site of the wound and the pearl-coloured corpse. The word "pearl", the drowning, and the water-words "floods", "washed", and "sea" suggest that Plath could have had in mind, "Those are pearls that were his eyes" from 'Ariel's Song' in Shakespeare's *The Tempest*; its first line, "Full fathom five thy father lies" may have come out of her frequent thoughts of her dead father.

Next, an entire ocean can revolve around one pocket in a reef, the way a person's life and all that it touches can centre around one hole made where the heart had been. Then, in short lines enhancing the smallness of the black-on-white image, the doom mark alive on minuscule legs makes the reader shudder beyond reason in the third stanza. Plath concludes 'Contusion' with three curt, linked sentences, loaded in their effect with despair and a giving up. (According to superstition, mirrors are sheeted after a death because someone who sees himself there will die next.)

In an incredible mood-change, the next day, 5th February, Plath wrote 'Balloons' with its child world, delightful and happy. As far removed from sentimentality as 'Contusion' that precedes it, and 'Edge', her final poem also written on 5th February, 'Balloons' may not go beyond description, but it is made up of non-stop metaphors and pared-down language – the essence of poetry. Plath gives the balloons their presence through well-observed shape, feel, sound, movement, and colour. Balloons do indeed shriek when grabbed, scoot when fleeing from the hand, and tremble at rest. There is not one word wasted in making a domestic picture. The baby, his jug-shaped body plumped on his bottom, takes in cause and effect – the pink world going clear, and the pink balloon condensing to red when it collapses.

Looking beyond Plath's poems, we find that some of her prose deserves to stand beside them, and that her life-story of zest and drive also claims attention. We have to be impressed by what she made of her experiences, stuffing those of the daylight into her prose in diverse ways, and certain others of the night into her poems. These latter she correctly believed would bring her fame.

A mystique has built up around her for good reasons. She was super-life-sized in her talents, ambition, and appetites, and a fruitful romance that turned harrowing. Confidence from early success, then the dramas around her and her magnetic husband, Ted Hughes, gave her glamour, added to by her good looks: tall and slim, she was highly attractive. The mystique lives on, kept alight by instances of genius in her poems, the later ones casting their baleful light upon her biography.

Still too close for perspective, perhaps more truly her story is too large. Few know that she was remarkable while growing up. From childhood on, while her creative self drew from its underground source, her rational self launched lightning strikes. She was published for the first time at eight years old. All through school she achieved top marks and won prizes and honours. She shone at everything she did. Besides, in her wanting to copy women in primitive cultures, powerful both at home as wife and mother and out in the world, she could be called a proto-feminist.

Nobody seems to write about Plath without pronounced feelings. This is a fitting response towards the young woman forever brim-full in her vibrant journals, letters to her mother, autobiographically-based short stories and novel, and in those poems where a different self goes boldly beyond our imagining. We keep looking for new revelations in the latest books about her, while continuing to sift through the familiar.

Today, the people she knew are old or dead. Her journals, recently published and coming into their own as literature, were cut short at the end – one missing, one destroyed. The book of her exuberant letters, slanted to please to begin with, has been edited to serve the ends of others. And her poems still challenge us from their fathoms, as they always will. This incompleteness only adds to the intrigue. Sylvia Plath has become personal to us through her story that sparkles with passion and word pictures. We want to know more.

1

Precocious Beginnings

To explain Plath's ambition that defines her almost as much as her talent, we should know first about her parents, both high achievers. She was trying to cope with how she felt about each of them for most of her short life.

Born in 1885 in Grabow, Germany, to a blacksmith-mechanic and his melancholic wife, Otto Platt emigrated at the age of 15 years to the USA. Changing his name to Plath, he worked in his uncle's Manhattan food and liquor store while auditing English classes. His English perfected in one year, he asked his Wisconsin grandfather, John, to pay for his education. John was willing if Otto would become a Lutheran minister. He agreed, but after graduating as a classical languages major, he saw the church's extreme conservatism too late, and quit the seminary. John excommunicated him from the family for not honouring their pact, striking his name from the Plath Bible.

For the next twenty workaholic years Otto travelled across the United States, studying and teaching German and biology (an interest gained from reading Darwin). With an MA, and graduate and faculty posts in five prestigious universities, he also acquired an MS and a PhD in science from Harvard. By 1922 he was teaching at Boston University, already recognised for his publications on the subject of bees. Then in 1929 his future wife, Aurelia Schober, half his age, entered one of his German classes as a graduate student.

Aurelia's father, Franz Schober, left Austria aged 14 and, after living near Venice, then in Paris, became a waiter in London.

One day he saw the picture of a colleague's young sister, a Viennese beauty named Aurelia. "I'll marry her," he boasted. Several years later, now calling himself Frank, he emigrated to Boston and became an accountant, living in his London friend's boarding house. One day the doorbell rang, and there stood Aurelia, more beautiful than in her picture. They married when she turned 18, and that year, 1906, Sylvia Plath's mother, also Aurelia, was born. They lived at the tip of the Winthrop Peninsula facing the Logan Airport, with the Atlantic Ocean behind.

Sylvia wrote about her childhood visits to their loved house in the beautiful 1962 essay, 'Ocean 1212-W' (her grandparents' phone number). At that early time and place she discovered the power of poetry when her mother read her a passage from Matthew Arnold's 'Forsaken Merman':

> I saw the gooseflesh on my skin. I did not know what made it. I was not cold. Had a ghost passed over? No, it was the poetry. A spark flew off Arnold and shook me, like a chill. I wanted to cry; I felt very odd. I had fallen into a new way of being happy.

There, after her brother's birth, she also discovered a lamentable human truth:

> As from a star I saw, coldly and soberly, the *separateness* of everything. I felt the wall of my skin: I am I. That stone is a stone. My beautiful fusion with the things of this world was over.

But to go back, young Aurelia hungrily read novels, her favourite writer being the poet, Emily Dickinson. Graduating first in her class in 1928, she planned to teach while getting a Master's degree. The German course in which she enrolled was taught by Otto, and an attraction led to marriage in January 1932.

Controlling every part of their lives and wanting to start a family right away, Otto asked her to resign her new, highly-promising teaching job. He also discouraged her from socialising, but she and her neighbour, Helen Hennessey, often strolled together with their baby-carriages. Helen Hennessey's daughter grew up to be Helen Vendler, well-known author of literary criticism.

Childhood

Otto and Aurelia's first baby, Sylvia, was born on Thursday, 27th October 1932. Easy, happy, and healthy, she was nursed on demand and cuddled when she cried. Her brother, Warren, was born in 1935. Sylvia would write of him later:

> Then there is your brother – 6 feet four inches tall, lovable and intelligent. You fought with him when you were little, threw tin soldiers at his head, gouged his neck with a careless flick of your iceskate … and then last summer, as you worked on the farm, you grew to love him, confide in him, and know him as a person … and you remember the white look of fear about his mouth that day they had all planned to throw you in the wash tub – and how he rallied to your defence.

In 1936, the family moved close to Boston Harbor, three miles north of Aurelia's parents. While Otto commuted, Aurelia read to Sylvia and Warren, starting with nursery rhymes and continuing through poems and fairy tales to A.A. Milne, J.R.R. Tolkien, Robert Louis Stevenson, Kipling, Lambs' *Tales from Shakespeare*, and with many more authors in between.

When young, Aurelia had wanted to be a writer. Her father disapproved, yet her talent proved useful. In 1932-1933 she helped Otto turn his dissertation into a trade book. His study in entomology, *Bumblebees and Their Ways*, published by Macmillan in 1934, became known around the world. Her work had been substantial and her writing made the book lively reading, but all Aurelia received was a routine acknowledgment for helping to edit and proofread. She also did most of the work for his 1935 essay on insect societies.

By that summer Otto had become thin, developed a sharp cough, and after teaching would collapse on the sofa, exhausted. As always, he refused to see a doctor, deducing that he had lung cancer. Treatment then was useless, and a swift death the best to hope for. As cancer carried a stigma (it was thought to be catching) he wished to die quietly and quickly, with no surgical 'butchering'.

With this background, Sylvia started school in 1937. Soon after she was keeping her first poems, formed and dated. On 21st September 1938, a notorious and devastating hurricane struck at five in the morning, to be mentioned later in 'Ocean 1212-W', 'The Daughters of Blossom Street', and several poems.

When Otto was home, the children stayed upstairs, coming down for half an hour in the evening to perform for him – singing a song, reciting a poem, or (in Sylvia's case) listing scientific names of insects by heart. Otto then gave each child a hug, and thus Sylvia learned early about getting attention and praise.

While Otto grew worse, Warren fell ill, so Sylvia was sent to the Schobers to relieve Aurelia in her constant nursing. Although she and her mother kept in touch daily by phone, they established at this time their habit of letter-writing, Aurelia always having stressed the importance of written expression.

In August 1940, Otto stubbed his toe, which caused an infected leg. Finally he let Aurelia call the doctor, who diagnosed advanced diabetes that could have been treated even up to a year previously. But now the disease moved quickly, ending in gangrene and the amputation of Otto's leg. A blood clot caused his death in the hospital at only 55. Sylvia's response, when Aurelia told her of his death, had been to say, "I'll never speak to God again."

Otto had always refused to take out health insurance, his life insurance had been spent on medical bills, and now their savings were gone. The Schobers moved in to help so that Aurelia could go back to teaching. By this time Sylvia thought of herself as a writer, her first published poem appearing in 1941.

President Roosevelt had kept the United States neutral while Hitler's Nazi Germany and Soviet Russia overran Poland in September 1939, and even when the Second World War had spread over Europe, and London was being blitzed by nightly bombing raids. But on 7th December 1941, when the Japanese attacked Pearl Harbour – a US Naval base on one of the Hawaiian Islands – America (joined by Britain) declared war on Japan, and then on

Germany and Italy on 11th December.

The war news did not affect the Plath children's high marks at school. They continued to excel even when Aurelia accepted a job teaching at Boston University in 1942, and moved the whole family to Wellesley, a college town on the Charles River, 45 miles west of Boston. Grandfather Frank now became a maître d'hôtel (after all, he'd been a waiter in London) and would bring home gourmet samplings that refined Sylvia's enthusiasm for food.

Plath became preoccupied with her father's death that seemed to her almost like a suicide. She couldn't understand how he, an internationally-known biologist, could have been so wrong. For her, many unresolved issues dated from the time of his death. Brought up as a Unitarian, Plath was to remain one, but she never looked there for comfort or answers.

Hard Work and Success

Right from the start, Plath established a pattern for hard work and success that won praise. Unfortunately, she never discovered whether or not she was still lovable if she achieved nothing, or failed, and it must be remembered that a person with drive may be driven. Because she was extremely bright and strong, she could count on being able to work hard and that it would pay off – her only future problems being sinus infections, premenstrual turmoil, and needing money. She would always expect to earn high marks, to be awarded honours, commendations, prizes, and distinctions, and to be published, which she went on to do.

While America was at war, insulated by distance, President Roosevelt dropped dead on 12th April 1945 during a portrait-painting session, and Vice President Harry Truman took over his office. On 7th May, Germany and Italy surrendered to the Allies. Atomic bombs were dropped on Hiroshima and Nagasaki, and Japan surrendered on 15th August.

Sylvia turned 13 with a big appetite for living – for food, boys, and writing. By the end of junior-high school in 1947, she had won many honours, one of which she was the only student in the school ever to earn, and she was placed first in a national art contest. By the time she entered high school in 1947, she was constantly sending stories and poems around to magazines while another part of her life was blossoming. She was becoming aware of sexuality. In her Journal she wrote about her gratitude to each of the 30 or 40 boys she had gone out with during the last two years for "an increased education in conversation, confidence and – so on."

She was busy in many areas. Having learned watercolour-painting, in the years thereafter she would make occasional little sketches to supplement her verbal pictures. Her drawings are strong, tight, detailed, and accurate. Two hard-edge, highly-stylised paintings, recently posted on the web, show confidence and skill. One self-portrait in pastel exists – youthful work that is amateurish compared to the others, but a fair likeness with an intent expression.

Loving classical music, she took a high school course in orchestra, and, having begun piano lessons around 1940, played it with much pleasure, although later dropped it for lack of time. She often mentioned Beethoven, and wrote her poem 'Little Fugue' having in mind his 'Grosse Fugue' from the late quartets.

By 1950, Plath had received 50 rejection slips for her writing before one acceptance. But in March she sold a teenage romance to *Seventeen* magazine, and her poem 'Bitter Strawberries' to the *Christian Science Monitor* – the first in a national publication. From then on she continued to be published. This mattered beyond giving her a name: it was a way to earn much-needed money in a time that included writing, studying, sports, acting a big part in a play, and attending formal dances and dinners. When she applied for admission to Smith College for women, one of the best in America, she was accepted, winning two scholarships. Plath graduated from high school first in her class, with all 'A's.

Now seriously lacking money, she took a summer job on a vegetable farm where an Estonian boy tried to seduce her. The essay she wrote about this, sugar-coated for her audience, was published in September. Another published story caused a college student, Eddie Cohen, to write her a fan letter. In the long correspondence that followed, Plath confided in him and he replied with important insights.

2

College Years

In the autumn of 1950, Sylvia Plath began her four years at Smith College. The feminist, Gloria Steinem, one of its alumnae from those days, reflected on how attending this prestigious institution meant filling in four years profitably enough before marriage, and how it nicely fitted in with a husband's needs. Smith was a good launching pad from which to look for a husband, with Harvard and Yale as the preferred targets. The students, many on blind dates, travelled to each others' campuses for football games, parties, and proms.

Premarital sex was taboo. Under the double standard, boys were tacitly encouraged to become experienced, while girls who gave in to their sexual feelings became known as 'fast' and lost their respectability. Boys and girls were now free to be alone together as never before (almost everyone owned or could borrow a car), but few could proceed to sexual fulfilment. Within more settled relationships, no one liked condoms, and no girl could obtain a diaphragm unless she was married or knew a broad-minded doctor. Until the Pill was available, mothers had to recommend marriage. Entries in Plath's journal show her bitterness at the double standard.

Women's position in the 1950s greatly preoccupied her; she often returned to it in her journal – how she could write while raising a family. She was determined to somehow manage. Then there was sex. With her robust appetites, Sylvia found chastity galling, and dreamed in rape fantasies of finding a man who could dominate her with a passion that matched her own.

At Smith, she wrote letters to her mother and Eddie Cohen,

studied hard, and occasionally dated. Fatigue brought about sinusitis leading to depression, but there was one high point: when the sponsor of her scholarship was revealed to her – Olive Higgins Prouty – Sylvia sent her a beautiful, moving letter of thanks, and a friendship followed with the older woman. Prouty was a successful writer, one of whose novels had been made into a film starring Bette Davis and Barbara Stanwyck, and the long-running radio serial, 'Stella Dallas'. She gave Plath advice on writing, which was to write about what you know: yourself. Plath had done this anyway, though worrying all the while that she should be writing about exotic subjects.

Mother

In *Letters Home* – edited who knows how much? – Plath sounds loving, confiding, and generally upbeat. While affectionate letters show affection, they can equally suggest a need to receive the same. In communicating events to her mother, she was also reaching out with her fervour for warmth:

> To have had you there in spirit! To have had you see me! I'm sure you would have cried for joy. That is why I am spilling out at such a rate – to try to share as much as I can with you.

A display of enthusiasm has many uses, all of which she must have known (Plath was said to be 'gushy'). It defends against melancholy by creating its own climate. It functions as a social suit of armour, deflecting hostility. And as a tried and true device, it draws benevolent attention.

Though one can't doubt Aurelia's generosity and affection, she seems to have been somewhat cold and not always understanding. Sylvia's approach to her was so habitual that she put on a perpetually bright manner with everyone.

The truth of this mother-daughter relationship was complex. Aurelia in many ways had been a fine role model, but when, at the end of 1958, the psychiatrist gave Sylvia permission to hate her, the negative underlay came surging up even while she acknowledged her due:

> Life was hell. She had to work. Work and be a mother too, a man and a woman in one sweet ulcerous ball. She pinched. Scraped. Wore the same old coat. But the children had ... piano lessons, viola lessons, French horn lessons ... they went to summer camp and learned to sail ... she worked to give those two innocent little children the world of joy she'd never had.

Whatever a mother does is inescapably magnified into great consequence for her children. Along with the omnipotence thrust upon her goes the fallibility; no human position is so fraught. Aurelia did her superb best (her son-in-law, Ted Hughes, became very fond and admiring of her), but the deadened aspects of her nature riled her sensitive daughter.

Furthermore, it is clear that she discouraged certain feelings and thoughts. "Now this is what I feel my mother felt ... I feel no love, only the Idea of Love, and that she thinks she loves me like she should. She'd do anything for me, wouldn't she?"

Eddie Cohen's and Plath's boss at *Mademoiselle* observed that Sylvia could never be spontaneous, a trait so pronounced that many people singled it out when describing her. "Mother with her usual miffed tragic look ... I could pass her in the street and not say a word, she depresses me so. But she is my mother." It reflected in contrived letter-writing constantly and at length from a young age. We should take note that home included the two people who had shaped her mother – her grandparents. Though much loved and kindly, they would have reinforced a strict German upbringing.

Since Plath died young, much of her biography naturally covers her relationship with her mother. In *The Bell Jar* she demonised the mother figure; after years of perfect behaviour she had many negative feelings to catch up on. Some of these she addressed in the poem 'The Disquieting Muses' (March 1958, according to the journals, but listed under 1957 in *The Collected Poems*). It combines the eerie figures with black shadows from a painting of that name by the surrealist, Giorgio de Chirico, with features of the fairy tale, *The Sleeping Beauty*, where the godmother not invited to a christening took revenge. As the poem begins, Sylvia asks her mother who had she failed to invite to her christening, which has caused these three ladies to stand around her crib nodding their darning-egg heads. (Darning eggs were hard oval forms pushed into the toes of socks to make mending their holes easier.) A trio that puts in mind the three witches in Shakespeare's *Macbeth* and the three Fates, they are here the bearers of featureless dread, the destructive, a disappointment, or a defeat that Aurelia refused to recognise.

Stanzas that follow narrate one instance of a hurricane's power unacknowledged, and two of Sylvia's failures and disappointments that followed from Aurelia's eternal optimism. The fourth stanza contains lovely images of light . The make-believe and the sparkle share something with the mirage stanza, "I woke one day…", except that here the lights are man-made (flashlight and twinkle dress), or bugs (fireflies and glowworms) – theatrics and the natural world – not just Aurelia's dreaming. Sylvia has had to face facts, such as having a wooden touch at the piano, despite her mother's relentless praise (stanza five).

The poem ends with two contrasting stanzas, the first a delicate, twittering, multi-coloured, millefleur fantasy in which her oblivious mother never touches the ground, but stays in air, enclosed in her iridescent bubble. The last shows the reality for Plath, forever grounded in an unchanging, monochrome-and-black surreal landscape without hope among the agents of her own bad-dreamworld. Plath will not, cannot tell her mother many truths, some of which lay under her baffling, blind depressions ever in the background. She will keep certain honest seeing to herself. Had she been able to share it, she might have lived to grow old.

The Journals

At age 11, Sylvia began journals and diaries whose pages were imprinted with dates. After 1945 she asked for the undated kind, saying that a single page was not enough for big moments. She kept some journals and notebooks simultaneously, as if she couldn't wait to express herself in the one not at hand.

Even before she turned 18, her entries engage us. She already took a professional attitude, noticing and recording, her larger-than-life appetite driving her to put down as much as possible. (Hence the idea that she had multiple selves – she wanted to make use of them all):

> Try always, as long as you have breath in your body, to take the hard way, the Spartan way – and work, work, work to build yourself into a rich, continually evolving entity!

Within the journals where she began to practise this, her handwriting connects to the determination in her character. The letters, clear, rounded, and four-square, with short upper strokes and downward tails, advance across the page in lines close together like a convoy of tiny, tightly-spaced Sherman tanks. Although the earliest entries are self-conscious explorations, clearly she was enjoying her craft. At first over-adjectival, but accurate, she described earnestly and well from an unedited array of selves. "Do I create?" she asked herself. "No, I reproduce." Always trying to be honest, she did not veer from anecdotes that showed her in a bad light:

> Jimmy Beal, who drew you pictures of pretty girls in fifth grade, and roller-skated along the beach and planned to get married in a little white house with roses on a picket fence – (you remember, absurdly now, how his little sister was drowned on the beaches while walking on ice cakes, and how you didn't know just how to react to this white, drawn face when you saw him back at school. You wanted to say nice things and how sorry you were, and then you felt a sudden hardening and strange anger at him for his weakness which intensified yours. So you stuck out your tongue at him and made a face. And you never played with him again.)

About her jealousy she was endearingly open:

> I am jealous of those who think more deeply, who write better, who draw better, who ski better, who look better, who live better, who love better than I.

Any dogged aspect at the journals' beginning is redeemed by enthusiasm and colour; then her writing becomes fluent, at her service, and poetry enters the prose. Rain, for instance, was plentiful by the coast and inland where she grew up, and she loved it for sight, sound, and variety:

> … the good rain coming down again – liquidly slopping down the shingled roof outside my window … spurting and drenching – and all the different timbers of tone – and syncopation.

She also loved the moon and its "dazzling drench of blue" on snow (entry later in England), different in her prose from the sinister, strange moon in her poems:

> … at midnight, when the moon makes blue lizard scales of roof shingles … So now I shall talk every night. To myself. To the moon. I shall walk, as I did tonight, jealous of my loneliness, in the blue-silver of the cold moon, shining brilliantly on the drifts of fresh-fallen snow, with the myriad sparkles.

Plath rolled up in her early paragraphs the sheen, taste, smell, glitter, sound, and feel – with a surround of thought and awareness in the Now – of the 1950s successful middle-class Ivy-League East-Coast America. Scenes and anecdotes merge to form autobiography as she wrote down what she felt and what preoccupied her (love, sex, marriage, and writing). By 1953 she knew that she could earn money by publishing:

> For three villanelles I have a blue-and-white pin-striped cotton cord suit dress, a black silk date dress and a grey raincoat with a frivolous pink lining.

Plath took a gloriously healthy approach towards food that

began early and shows up over and over in her entries as an inevitable part of experiences:

> ... Spooned up watery red soup ... Then the uncuttable tough florid-pink tongue, the watery orange turnip, mashed potato, slippery dressinged lettuce, lucent & fresh as a drink of water ...

She listed what was served at dinners, hers and her hosts, and the cakes and pies she baked for Ted, who had a sweet-tooth.

Hughes said that she only became herself a few months before she died. She seemed, however, to have been always presenting each self as it came up, not keeping any back in the interest of consistency.

There is a charming poem, called 'Geography Lesson', by the 18-year-old Sylvia (with her spelling) from the (April) 1951 Journal, "Written, as usual, in the tense and crucial interval when I should be studying for a Botany exam". Left out of *The Collected Poems*, it should not be missed.

Further Successes

By 1951 Plath had published enough for a newspaper to run a biographical article on her. She kept up her excellent marks in spite of bad colds and depression, fatigue taking its toll as she lived hard and sometimes high – such as when, in October, she and the other housemates of Maureen Buckley were invited to her coming-out party in Sharon, Connecticut. The Buckleys, a family of great prominence and wealth, sent Cadillacs to transport everyone to Sharon for the night and back the following day.

As Plath studied, took a job to augment her earnings from publishing, and dated men besides her boyfriend, Dick Norton (a medical student at Yale, then Harvard), she again became depressed. She wrote about it to Eddie, who put it plainly that she was deceiving herself about loving Dick, and also needed sexual satisfaction. He had been the first to suggest she see a psychiatrist for her depressions and, after visiting her, to notice "that she seemed incapable of an impulsive remark", that she was "all mask" (as Ted Hughes later observed, also).

If Plath looked for help about spiritual matters in her reading, it led to myth with its poetic idea of death leading to rebirth. In her more personal beliefs, she, formerly a self-styled atheist while being a Unitarian, referred to herself in a college paper on Unitarianism as an "agnostic humanist".

In the spring of 1952, she wrote a short story, 'Sunday at the Mintons' – the characters based on herself and Dick, who the protagonist kills in her head – and it won a $500 first prize in a contest run by *Mademoiselle.* This eased her money worries for the time until she lost her summer job as a waitress: because she worked all day and went out with men until dawn, she had to go home to recover from infected sinuses. A letter from Knopf's editor-in-chief cheered her; he had read her prize-winning story and wanted her to think of writing a novel.

Plath returned to her overly-full junior year at Smith hoping to attend Oxford or Cambridge after graduation. Marriage could wait, and it would not be to Dick. Adding to the general praise for her 'Sunday at the Mintons', an editor from Dodd, Mead, showed interest in her writing them a novel, too. Literary successes (though still not with *The New Yorker*, most desired) encouraged her to try for a guest editorship with *Mademoiselle* in Manhattan for the next summer.

1953 began with meeting more boys, including Gordon Lameyer, who became important to her; further poems published; and winning her guest editorship. *Mademoiselle* then asked her to write a profile of the Irish writer, Elizabeth Bowen, and an article titled 'Poets on Campus' about five young poets – George Steiner, William Burford, Alastair Reid, Anthony Hecht, and Richard Wilbur. She already knew Wilbur through his mother-in-law, Edna Ward, a friend of Aurelia's. (Later, Ward was to invite Aurelia and Sylvia to tea during her depression in hopes that Wilbur could help by talking to her. He wrote a fine and moving poem about the occasion, 'Cottage Street, 1953'.)

Plath ended the school year first in her class, with two important poetry prizes.

New York

In the summer of 1953, along with 19 other guest editors, she was lodged by *Mademoiselle* at the plush, old Barbizon Hotel for women in Manhattan. Each girl was then assigned to an editor in order to learn about one department. Although Plath had asked to work in fiction, she had been placed under the managing editor, Cyrilly Abels, as guest managing editor during the tightly-programmed stay. When she wasn't working on articles, or reading manuscripts (and rejecting a manuscript of someone on the staff of *The New Yorker*, which must have given her a sweet moment) she was being photographed (holding a rose, etc.), or was attending a fashion show, a formal dance at the St Regis Hotel, the ballet, the theatre, a baseball game at Yankee Stadium, another dance, a cocktail party, a movie first-night, and a crabmeat luncheon that made all the guest editors sick for two days with ptomaine poisoning. Otherwise, she met some key literary people, dated a friend who was an interpreter at the UN, toured other magazine offices and the *Herald Tribune*, visited a noted hat establishment (women wore gloves and a hat to the office), bars, Greenwich Village, and Macy's department store – and got lured into a few adventures on the side. When, in mid-June, her brother Warren graduated from Exeter with a scholarship to Harvard, Sylvia didn't have enough money for the trip to his commencement, but anyway needed to catch up on her work at *Mademoiselle*.

Not surprisingly she became exhausted, which sometimes made her act strangely, such as when she missed meeting Dylan Thomas by being away from her desk, she spent several days trying to run into him. An event that troubled her profoundly was the imminent execution by electric chair of Ethel and Julius Rosenberg for spying for the Soviet Union. The day it was scheduled, she was too upset to eat breakfast, comparing the fried eggs to what was about to happen to the Rosenbergs. One of the other guest editors recalled later that Plath's skin broke out in red patches, mimicking burns on the hour she believed that the execution was taking place. A last instance of extravagant behaviour was throwing all of her clothes off the hotel roof in a gesture of disgust at her visit (and therefore needing to borrow a skirt and blouse on the day she went home.) That certain episodes had disappointed, disillusioned, and on some level wounded her, she saw as her own failure, and as her having failed everybody.

Depression and Attempted Suicide

Plath had hoped to attend a writing workshop given by Frank O'Connor at Harvard Summer School, but she arrived home to the news that she had not been accepted, a blow she could scarcely handle. This came on top of intense fatigue and her reaction to the New York scene. She became depressed to the point of wanting to die. When she told her mother, Aurelia sought advice from a psychiatrist who prescribed electroshock therapy.

The procedure was barbaric. Sylvia was given no muscle relaxant, or anaesthesia, or company during recovery, all of which soon became standard. Added to this was month-long insomnia. Although Plath appeared her usual self, on 24th August she decided she would no longer endure her life. When everyone was out of the house, she left a note saying that she had gone for a walk and would be home the next day, hid in a crawl space under the front porch, and swallowed forty sleeping pills.

Aurelia, out with some friends, suddenly felt an unaccountable dread. She rushed home, found the note, and immediately telephoned the police. The story of Sylvia's disappearance and the hunt for her went nationwide through the papers. Down in the cellar two days later, Grammy Schober heard a moan, and thus Sylvia was found. Her having taken too many pills saved her life because she vomited them up. She was in fair condition, but a piece of concrete had raked her right cheek, and the wound that afterwards left a scar caused high fever.

Meanwhile, her sponsor, Prouty, especially sympathetic because of her own breakdown years ago, heard the story through the media. She lost no time in offering Aurelia help. Taking charge, she got Sylvia the best medical care available, first at the Massachusetts General Hospital, then at a connected mental hospital, McLean. Plath was assigned to a young woman psychiatrist who was ahead of her time, Dr Ruth Beuscher, someone Sylvia looked up to, was to remain in touch with, and see on and off in the future. Dr Beuscher found her full of anger, much of it directed at her mother. She felt that her emotions had never counted, and that performance at school had meant everything. Moreover, her stay in Manhattan had been traumatic.

Plath needed to be hospitalised until early January of 1954. She improved quickly after receiving properly administered shock treatments that Dr Beuscher had readied her for. Then, on a visit home just before being released, she initiated her first sexual intercourse at age 21 with a boy she'd known since the ninth grade. (After the second encounter they decided to revert to their former platonic friendship.) Dr Beuscher had given her a prescription for a diaphragm and recommended its use for her health.

Around this time Aurelia heard from a sister of Otto that Sylvia's depression was likely congenital. Three female members of Otto's family had suffered from it, and it had caused his mother to be hospitalized.

Men and Sex

In February of 1954, Plath returned to Smith and soon was writing and being published again. A friendship developed with a girl named Nancy Hunter, to whom she could confide her feelings about her father for the first time. Nancy remembered her calling him autocratic, saying that she adored and hated him and probably had wished him dead. When he died, she felt she had killed him.

Regarding men, she was honest and astute about herself:

> The old, primal hate. That desire to go around castrating the arrogant ones who become such children at the moment of passion … I hated men because they didn't stay around and love me like a father … I made them propose and then showed them they hadn't a chance.

At the same time, she needed them:

> Oh, I would like to get in a car and be driven off into the mountains to a cabin on a wind-howling hill and be raped

> in a huge lust like a cave woman, fighting, screaming, biting in a ferocious ecstasy of orgasm …

In March she visited New York and dated new boys. One, of significance, was Richard Sassoon (related to the English poet, Siegfried Sassoon), a sexy, cultivated, sophisticated Englishman, born in Paris. Again, corresponding with Eddie Cohen, she asked for her old letters back to use for a short story. Typically incisive, he replied that his letters were worth more than hers, not as literature, but for truths he told her about herself. He added that she was "no more capable of giving in anger than giving in love", both needed for her to become whole.

At the end of the school year, besides winning money for a prize poem, Plath received the largest scholarship Smith could award for the coming year, plus a scholarship to Harvard Summer School. She returned home for the summer with her hair dyed platinum blonde (jolting her mother). After hectic socialising, she left for Harvard Summer School, renting an apartment in Boston with Nancy Hunter and two other girls. Eager for experience, she dated a professor she and Nancy had picked up. He raped her, causing her to haemorrhage seriously, needing to go to the hospital. Yet she kept on dating him as well as Lameyer, now serious about marrying her.

Back in Smith for her senior year, Plath applied for graduate work at Oxford and Cambridge – for the interviews dyeing her newly platinum-blonde hair a dark brown in order to appear serious. Her creative writing course was taught that year by the writer, Alfred Kazin, whom she impressed. By now, the rather exotic Richard Sassoon had begun to interest her, and she spent a weekend in New York with him.

That she kept seeing a man who had raped her, that she remained fascinated for a long time by Sassoon who slapped and spanked her, and that she eventually married a man with a truly violent streak, causes speculation about her sexuality: she must have sought out violence in hopes of finding release. (In time, suicide became the ultimate violence.) She – so disciplined in her habits that she astonished Nancy at her meticulous arrangement and storage of clothes – craved rough treatment to find a way beyond her tight self. She replied when asked about her clothing, "Yes, if anyone ever disarranged my things I'd feel as though I'd been raped intellectually". That her sexuality simmered together with the idea of rape and violence came through in other remarks, too.

An episode in the summer of 1949 had made this connection. A car crash that she had secretly wished for at the stockcar races, with seven people taken away in ambulances, was closely followed by a frantic necking session with her escort in his car.

A Portrait

As expected, from Plath's letters of recommendation for graduate schools and scholarships: " … I have never had a more brilliant and a more charming student to teach", and " … the outstanding student in my experience at Smith College …" Her housemother filed a more nitty-gritty evaluation in the Vocational Office: " … unquestionable character … her appearance is quite striking. She has a pleasant voice and pleasing, correct deportment. [But she] is self-cantered and very selfish. Her talent for writing has made her difficult for the girls to live with."

From her biographies we can imagine that she was an animated, somewhat jangling presence. Jealousy, her worst fault, came from pressure to be perfect or, at least, better than everyone else. From her writing we know that she was observant about others, but in some ways perhaps insensitive ('pushy') because blinded by inner needs. Even as a so-called charmer, she evidently projected a poisonous presence when angry. From Ted Hughes' book of poems, *Birthday Letters*: "lip-gnawing scowl" and "homicidal hooded stare". Diane Middlebrook, in her masterful biography, *Her Husband*, calls her "opinionated, impatient, sometimes arrogant, and always on the move" – probably the best summing up – and records the writer Doris Lessing's phrase, Plath's "incandescent desperation", which showed how vulnerable she really was.

There exists a telling (and touching) appendix to her published Journals – her "Back to School Commandments" (prefaced by three rules, the first being "I will not overwhelm him by breathless over-enthusiasm"!). The first commandment is (her capitalisation): "Keep a CHEERFUL FRONT continuously"; the last " … KEEP CHEERFUL …" As for wearing masks, she wrote at a bad time: "Masks are the order of the day – and the least I can do is cultivate the illusion that I am gay, serene, not hollow and afraid." In keeping with her carefulness, she had drawn up a list for how to conduct herself, such as "Be friendly & more subdued"; "Don't blab too much"; "Keep troubles to self"; "Bear mean gossip & snubbing & pass beyond it – be nice & positive to all".

At Cambridge, she was described as "nice, bright, neat, gushy" (Hughes wrote, "gushy burblings" in *Birthday Letters*). Added to which would be *clean*, cleanliness being something super-important to her. Someone commented on her lack of smell, an American trait noticeable among the less deodorised. *Flashy* is another word that the British used. She arrived with gold and white Samsonite suitcases, and her clothes-style (she enjoyed clothes) made her look over-dressed in England. Red was her favourite colour and her frequent choice – fire-engine red – the red of her lipstick, of her shoes and hair-band the night she met Ted Hughes, although, a few months before she died, she wrote, "Blue is my new color, royal, midnight … Ted never liked blue, and I am a really blue-period person now".

No one could photograph her intensity and animation, considered by Hughes to be her greatest beauty and he thought her dark-brown eyes particularly expressive. Perhaps because of the spirit within, her skin had a special sheen. She wore thick, bright red lipstick on a full-lipped, mobile mouth, and her smile dazzled although when listening she scowled in concentration. Photographs of her modelling a bathing suit show her as slender, with long, slim legs. She stood at five feet nine inches, and weighed 137 pounds (measurements in the Smith office) with a build judged to be perfect. Her voice, clear and assured, had good enunciation softened by a few traces of Boston and British, and a not-unpleasant, slightly penetrating quality.

To bring some three-dimensionality to her presence, here are other observations. Mallory Wober, a young male friend at

Cambridge, said that she always attracted looks and that she lived with a genius' intensity. Cyrilly Abels, the formidable Managing Editor at *Mademoiselle* – "I never found anyone so unspontaneous so consistently, especially in one so young. She was simply all façade, too polite, too well-brought-up and well-disciplined". A friend and competitor at Cambridge, Jane Kopp – she "always dressed in the *Mademoiselle* idea of American couture". A. Alvarez, poetry editor of *The Observer* – "briskly American, bright, clean, competent, like a young woman in a cookery advertisement".

Having been too thoroughly regulated, Plath showed no tendency to rebel, to identify with outsiders and wild ones, or even seek ivory-tower elitism. For her, used to success and inclined towards perfection, this left the norm.

She omitted her saving grace, a sense of humour, seeing herself this way:

> I have a good self, that loves skies, hills, ideas, tasty meals, bright colors. My demon would murder this self by demanding it be a paragon, and saying it should run away if it is being anything less. I shall doggedly do my best and know it for that, no matter what other people say.

> I am, at bottom, simple, credulous, feminine & loving to be mastered, cared for – but I will kill with my mind, my ice-eye, anyone who is weak, false, sickly in soul ...

Last Term

In 1955, a severe sinus infection began Plath's last term, landing her in the infirmary where she wrote poems and received visitors. One, sent by Alfred Kazin, was Peter Davison from Harcourt, Brace – a graduate of Harvard and Cambridge, young, handsome, attractive, and a poet (later, poetry editor of *The Atlantic Monthly*). Once recovered, she finalised her thesis on Dostoevsky, called a "masterpiece" by her professor. In February, she learned that both Oxford and Cambridge had accepted her, and in the spring, she won a truly impressive series of awards and prizes besides a Fulbright Fellowship to Cambridge.

Plath graduated summa cum laude and received two further awards. Adlai Stevenson (Governor of Illinois, and failed presidential candidate) gave the commencement speech, saying that the girls' "highest vocation" would be to attain a "creative marriage". Long afterwards, one girl said that thanks to their years at Smith they didn't actually believe this – until they found it happening.

During Plath's remaining time in America she saw Lameyer and Sassoon, and enjoyed an affair with Peter Davison, going to parties with him before brushing him off. More poems were published, and an agent representing the writers Saul Bellow and Thomas Wolfe contacted her. Then, in mid-September she sailed for England.

3

Cambridge

Predictably, Plath had a shipboard romance that extended to a few days in London before she settled, in October 1955, near Newnham, her college in Cambridge. She made friends without delay and began a busy term, studying, writing, and publishing. When in January 1956 she heard that back in Wellesley her loved Grammy was diagnosed with stomach cancer, her recent depression deepened. In February, bad reviews of her poems appeared in the Cambridge literary journal, *Chequer*.

Learning that a new journal, *The St Botolph's Review*, was to be launched with a party on 25th February, she gladly planned to go. She had read a copy and, finding poems there of power and truth by E. Lucas Myers and Ted Hughes (she liked his for their violence), wanted to meet them both.

Wearing silver earrings and a red headband to match her red shoes, she and a friend arrived at the party, already blurred by alcohol. First she confronted Daniel Huws, author of her bad review in *Chequer*, and then she danced with Myers, telling him how much she liked his poems and quoting one. And then, spotting a "big, dark, hunky boy, the only one … huge enough for me" across the room, she knew that she had to meet him. He noticed her, and as he came towards her, his eyes fixed on hers, she knew that this was Ted Hughes. Prepared, she quoted one of his poems at him. "You like?" he asked. In a side room where they chatted and drank together, he suddenly kissed her "bang smash on the mouth", and tore off her hair band and earrings, saying, "Hah, I shall keep." When he kissed her neck, she bit his cheek, making blood run down.

Within two days she produced the exciting tour-de-force poem, 'Pursuit', written in one afternoon, worked over the next, and considered finished. Here the man, the animal, and sexual desire are all one in pursuit of the prey that is both desired and desiring. The trance-inducing rhythm likens to an animal padding right behind as close as a pounding heartbeat.

Sometimes consonants are repeated as in Anglo-Saxon poetry (for example, the repeated ***h***s in the first line of the fourth stanza), and sometimes vowels (note the repeated double ***e*** in the fifth line of the second stanza). Both types of repetition help bind the poem together and make it sing. 'Pursuit' is a direct metaphor, much more extended and specific than William Blake's 'The Tiger'. Third in *The Collected Poems*, this outpouring seems to have been facilitated by Plath's having written the first, 'Conversation Among the Ruins', that begins with imagery of stalking and wildness and contains some of the same words and character.

If parts appear a little rough (stanza 1, line 7 is an awkward mouthful although the imagery works well), and over-the-top, this is in keeping with its authentic, feverish character. Some readers consider this poem her best.

Little did Plath know how well 'Pursuit' would fit Ted Hughes, an experienced hunter of game – and of women.

Ted Hughes, known as the biggest seducer in Cambridge, remembered her. She worried that he might not have, though. To get her attention the night after the party, he threw clods at the wrong window, but she finally heard of his attempts to contact her. Then Myers invited her, on her way to Paris for the spring break, to stop off at the London flat that he and Ted were briefly using. She did so, and she and Hughes made love. In Paris, hoping but failing to find Sassoon (while sightseeing with three other men), she met Gordon Lameyer, and they travelled, quarrelling, to Germany, Austria, Venice, and Rome before parting, barely friends. She then returned to London.

Ted Hughes

The American writer, Ben Sonnenberg, said about Hughes in the 1960s: "I felt like Hazlitt meeting Coleridge for the first time: bowled over by his warmth and energy." As described by Plath, he had "a voice like the thunder of God" that "boomed through walls and doors". "Such violence … the one man in the room who was as big as his poems, huge, with hulk and dynamic chunks of words … oh, to give myself crashing, fighting to you." She called him "a breaker of things and people." Their first night of love-making left her with a "battered face, smeared with a purple bruise … and my neck raw and wounded too."

From Hughes' own poem, 'Macaw and Little Miss', the lines describing a warrior's sexual violence seem to apply to himself most aptly. In spite of his old clothes, greasy hair, and dandruff (remarks about his personal hygiene were legion), he had sexual magnetism and presence – a dimension that Sylvia lacked. Yet even while enjoying fame, he seems to have remained essentially a private person.

Ted Hughes was born in August 1930 in Yorkshire. His father, William, a carpenter, then shopkeeper, had been awarded a Distinguished Conduct Medal for acting with great courage during the First World War. Ted's forceful mother, Edith Farrar, who descended from notable ancestors, studied magic; his interest in stories as spoken and in the occult came from her. His much older brother, Gerald, who moved to Australia, had taught him hunting, shooting, trapping, and fishing (which Ted was to mythologize). Olwyn, his older sister, worked in Paris, and in time became the agent for the Sylvia Plath estate.

A group of Ted's poems won him entrance to Pembroke College at Cambridge, which he attended after serving as a ground wireless mechanic in the RAF in the north Yorkshire moors (with time to read the Bible and Shakespeare). Since graduating in 1954, he had been a gardener, a night watchman and, at the time he met Plath, was adapting fiction for screenplays at J. Arthur Rank's Pinewood Studios. In his hours off he was the centre of a group of old friends who drank in a Cambridge pub and contributed to literary magazines. One was the new *The St Botolph's Review*, named for Luke Myers' digs, a converted chicken coop behind St Botolph's Rectory, barely large enough for a bed and a desk. When visiting, Ted stayed there, too.

He seems to have provoked ambivalent feelings in Sylvia from as early as their honeymoon, and eyebrows must have been raised when in her short story, 'The Fifty-Ninth Bear', she killed him off. While his shortcomings were linked with three major tragedies (including the death of his and Assia Wevill's baby, Shura), he never took advantage of Sylvia's being a woman to put her in second place. He helped ensure her equal time for writing. After her death, he spent the rest of his life in a literary commitment to her – which begot him a fortune – while many women came and went.

Wedding and Honeymoon

In the spring of 1956, Plath attended lectures and spent time with Hughes. As his self-designated literary agent, she typed up his poems and ran an organised mail campaign to get him into print. On the strength of having been published by the Cambridge *Varsity*, she was able to attend the highly-publicised London reception on 24th April for Bulganin (then Prime Minister of the Soviet Union) and Khrushchev (then First Secretary of the Communist Party), on a tour together that was referred to by the Press as "the B and K show". In a letter home, Plath described Bulganin – "a dear, white-bearded little man with clear blue eyes", and followed that with, "I found myself shaking his hand and begging, 'Please do come to visit Cambridge' ".

Meanwhile, Plath's supervisor had been sending her Smith professor, Mary Ellen Chase, reports on her outstanding work. Chase, visiting Cambridge, had coffee with Plath and mentioned that Smith might offer her a teaching job.

After Grammy's death, Aurelia sailed to London and found her daughter and Hughes planning marriage. Finding him charming, she cooperated, and the wedding took place with Aurelia there on the rainy afternoon of 16th June. Sylvia wore a pink hair-ribbon and a pink knitted suit fortuitously brought by her mother as a present, and carried a pink rose given her by Ted.

Then, all three travelled to Paris, and while Aurelia toured Europe alone, Sylvia and Ted went on to Benidorm on Spain's east coast for their honeymoon. A "small village bordering on a peacock-blue bay. Its white pueblos shone like salt crystals in the sun" – Benidorm comes to colourful life in Plath's notebooks and her short story, 'That Widow Mangada'.

'Fiesta Melons' shows how, with her word-sense and artist's eye for shapes and colours – bright and dark green, pink, and orange – Plath made them physical, with sound in the word "thumpable" that appears in the fifth line. Notice all the ***o***s and short, strong words that mimic the melon shapes, like the verb "bowl" (followed by "***o***ne h***o***meward" with more ***o***s) adds roundness and weight to the "ovals" and "balls". There are cooling, soothing ***m***, ***n***, and ***oo*** sounds for the "cream-smooth honeydews", then a change of texture with syllables made abrupt by ***p***s in the next two lines. The sound of the adjective "bump" brings it to life as a verb, making the melons even more 3-D. The sound of knocking a melon to test its ripeness echoes in "Pink-pulped whoppers".

Although her speciality was cakes, Plath now learned with great gusto to cook tortillas and delicious meals on a one-gas burner:

> … dishes are washed in cold water with tangles of straw;
> and a one-ring petrol stove must cope with everything from
> *café con leche* to rich rabbit stew.

While she and Hughes kept up working habits that made their relationship unique – writing for set hours each day together, and giving each other ideas, encouragement, and criticism – there are signs that the high point of their happiness had passed. Plath's poem, 'The Other Two', reveals instances of misery mirrored in the enormous walnut table in their rented villa.

Running out of money, they left for Paris where they met Sylvia's brother, Warren, then visited Ted's parents in Yorkshire, who only then learned that he was married. Here, they took walks on the moors and kept up their writing schedules, while Plath typed and circulated their manuscripts.

Back in Cambridge, they moved into a flat where the one bathroom was shared with Siegfried Sassoon's son and his wife upstairs. Plath confidently submitted Hughes' poetry manuscript of *The Hawk in the Rain* to a contest run by the Poetry Center of the 92nd Street 'Y' in New York City, the winner to be picked by Marianne Moore, Stephen Spender, and W.H. Auden, and published by Harper and Brothers. At this time money was desperately short. And, ominously, a letter of Richard Sassoon's comments on how unhappy Plath seemed to be in her marriage. But February of 1957 brought two pieces of good news. Hughes won the contest, and Plath was offered a job at Smith.

In the spring, while she wrote and studied for her final exams, Faber & Faber, with a letter of congratulations from T.S. Eliot, also took Hughes' *The Hawk in the Rain*, soon to be published in England and honoured by The Poetry Book Society as its autumn choice. Then, Sylvia's final exams behind her, Ted marked their first wedding anniversary by hauling an enormous vase of pink roses into the bedroom.

4

Smith, Boston, England

> … writing makes me a small god: I re-create the flux and smash of the world through the small ordered word-patterns I make …

In June of 1957, before beginning her job, Sylvia introduced Ted to relatives and old friends at a reception given by Aurelia in Wellesley. Once at Smith, she found her three Freshman English classes hard work and the other teachers unfriendly in contrast to her student days there. ("All the faces of my student shining days turned the other way.") Before, she had been writing and getting published; now she was overtired, scarcely able to write at all. Another problem surfaced: Ted was seen strolling with attractive, blonde students. A girl from one of Sylvia's classes later spoke her mind about this, saying that her students felt "tremendously protective" of her, and that this was "rather rotten", his embarrassing her publicly when they were newly married.

Life for Hughes now was a string of successes (including a publication in *The New Yorker*) while Plath couldn't write. Whereas in the past she used to worry about outstripping a future husband, now, at least, she was relieved of this problem (had she pushed him ahead to avoid it?) and was, so far, not eaten by jealousy of Hughes' fame. From her journal:

> Luckily he [Ted] is ahead of me so far I never need fear the old superiority heel-grinding … Must work & get out of paralysis … Smile, write in secret, showing no one. Amass a great deal. Novel. Poems. Stories. Then send about. Let no book-wishing show – work. I must move

> myself first, before I move others – a woman famous among women.

Before the Christmas vacation she fell ill with viral pneumonia. After a long spell of writer's block and little published, in March of 1958 Plath wrote eight poems (in eight days) inspired by paintings, which restored her faith in herself, although she still came down with bad colds:

> … Ted, who is as close & warm & dear as can be, closer, warmer, dearer than I ever was to myself – who sees me sick, ugly, sallow, sneezy & hugs me, holds me, cooks me a veal chop & brings bowls of iced pineapple, steaming coffee at breakfast, tea at teatime.

Her last term – she had turned down a renewal for the next year – was not happy. She and Ted were quarrelling. After her last class, when he was supposed to meet her, she saw him with a pretty student who ran off as she approached.

> Love has been an inexhaustible spring for my nourishment and now I gag.

One fight left her having seen stars from being hit, and with a sprained thumb, and Ted with scratches on his face.

From Plath's journals, some concise and often devastating thumbnail sketches of people she saw those days show her talent for verbal caricature. She was kind to those she liked, but when the journals were published, certain ones – see the complete text – must have had highly ambivalent reactions to being memorialised here ("I … won't waste poem-time on people I can't stand").

> Mrs Van der Poel … her heels high, her fur opulent, a highly trained poodle with a taste for modern art … One suspects her dry bright tidy little voice could find a lucid epithet for the worst chaos.

> Paul, with his professional dewy blue eyed look and his commercially gilded and curled blond hair on his erect, dainty-boned aristocrat head looking as if it had been struck on a Greek coin that since had blurred and thinned from too much public barter and fingering ...

> Truman Capote ... a baby-boy, must be in his middle thirties. Big head, as of a prematurely delivered baby, an embryo, big white forehead, little drawstring mouth, shock of blonde hair, mincy skippy fairy body in black jacket ...

In a gamble Aurelia disapproved of, they decided to spend a year writing in Boston without jobs. Plath, writing again, at last received her first acceptance from *The New Yorker* for two poems, with a warm note from Howard Moss and a cheque that covered three months rent. But soon she found it hard to write and was slipping into another depression. Worried about money, in October she took a secretarial job for two months at the Massachusetts General Hospital's adult psychiatric clinic where she had been hospitalised before. Her best short story was written around this time, 'Johnny Panic and the Bible of Dreams', which made use of her experiences in the hospital. She returned to Dr Beuscher for regular sessions, too. This opened up the subject of her relationship with her mother – she wondered why she felt unloved by her when all evidence showed the contrary. Plath also examined her marriage, concluding that Hughes knew she loved him but let her down, as she felt her father had.

Often, womanisers and those who express a grand concern with sex substitute genital activity for heart feelings, and confuse marathons of pumping for making love. Endurance kings or queens, they merely couple, their emotionally numb staying-power replacing effective union and contributing to problems never defined, such as an insufficient climax. They, unlike lovers nourished by intimacy, are apt to leave a wreckage of relationships behind.

In spite of all her references to making love, Plath never wrote a single love poem. (Diane Middlebrook points out that food, not sex, was a primary topic.) The poem to Hughes in her *Collected*

Poems is a self-conscious use of hyperbole to say what she *thought* about him. The other poems about him are stricken with pain. Although her liking for rape and violence may have conflated with Hughes' violent streak into romantic excitement for a spell, persons capable of satisfying sexual release do not seek violence in sex, nor do their personalities project violence. As things were, any long-term relationship for Plath and Hughes would seem to have been doomed.

Encouraged by Dr Beuscher, Plath visited her father's grave on 8th March 1959 for the first time, and was overwhelmed by the strength of her rage and grief, feelings that were to surface in many poems and in her marriage.

Plath and Hughes continued writing, publishing, and entertaining. In Robert Lowell's creative writing class in the spring of 1959, Plath became friends with the poets Anne Sexton and Sexton's friend, George Starbuck. Sexton had been a mental patient, and she and Plath were able to talk about their suicidal feelings.

The Short Stories

> I have experienced love, sorrow, madness, and if I can not make these experiences meaningful, no new experience will help me.

The subjects of her short stories are the familiar. Plath, with aspirations to write for "the slicks", believed in fulfilment through day-to-day experiences. (Her own goal was marriage and a family, though with writing on the side.) Studded with adjectives, her short stories use large cross-sections of autobiography practically unaltered, except for directions they may take. They contain something of her drawings and her handwriting – a *square* quality. As they begin, everything is level with the true-to-life – not taller, not wider, nothing deeper – our daily bread as raw material. Scenes are upholstered with details that lull us into comfortable hyper-normality; then comes the little twist:

> A snowdrift of currant cakes and buttered scones banked the blue-willow platter and the little cut-glass bowl held generous dollops of Nellie Meehan's homemade gooseberry jam. Outside, in the clear, windy night, the moon shone high and full; a blue, luminous mist was rising from the bottom of the valley where the mountain stream flowed black and deep over those foaming falls in which Dora's brother-in-law had chosen to drown himself a week ago come Monday. ['All the Dead Dears']

In one long, wry sentence she could telescope a couple's fate:

> And as at the wave of a wand, the beaming Regans were whisked from an unheated, cold-water flat and a diet of spaghetti and potato soup into the luxuriant green pastures of Kensington with a backdrop of vintage wines, sports cars, chic furs and, ultimately, the more somber décor of the divorce courts. ['Day of Success']

Even where no poetry lights the prose, a poetic mind casts the story, no matter how slight. Yet poetry and Plath's painting eye are often present, too. Her descriptions create a series of still lives in primary colours, bright and distinct, where nothing is too small for its exact designation:

> Hamish dropped the match to the ground. He crushed it under his foot. The small yellow world went out and the courtyard flowered, large, luminous, blue in the light of the moon.

'Johnny Panic and the Bible of Dreams', haunting and horrible, ends:

> The air crackles with his blue-tongued lightning-haloed
> angels.
> His love is the twenty-story leap, the rope at the throat,
> the knife at the heart.
> He forgets not his own.

Literary Life

Plath (who in her journal had listed her rivals from Sappho on through) began to feel jealous of Sexton and Starbuck, although she continued to publish and Heinemann showed interest in a prospective book of poems. Despite her 1950s' view that men come first, when she failed to write as well as she knew she could, if at all, and Hughes was lionized from all quarters, she finally admitted to being jealous of him, too. (A short story, 'The Wishing Box', is about her jealousy of his interesting dreams. She was always open about what she felt.)

In April 1959 Hughes learned he'd won a Guggenheim grant. Because of Plath's bad feelings and Hughes' increasing unhappiness in America, they decided to move to England after a tour of America and a three-month stay writing poetry at Yaddo, an artists' residence in Saratoga Springs, New York.

Plath was pregnant when they settled in a London flat in February 1960, very near the poet W.S. Merwin and his wife Dido, and began a strenuous social life with old friends and the literary crowd. Someone remarked how impressive they were, very tall and good-looking like a pair of gods. Heinemann gave Plath a book contract for her collection of poems, called *The Colossus*, to be dedicated to Ted. And Faber and Faber issued Hughes' book of poems, *Lupercal*, dedicated to Sylvia, which received wildly-favourable reviews that won him the Somerset Maugham Award. They both met A. Alvarez, poetry editor of the *Observer*, who interviewed Hughes and found him as striking as his poems. He had accepted a poem of Plath's a year earlier, but needed to be reminded of who she was.

New Family

On 1st April 1960, Sylvia gave birth at home to their daughter Frieda, with Ted and a midwife attending. 'Morning Song' is for her. The poem, starting from the baby's first cry, gently proceeds through the experience of being faced with a newborn in their midst, to the lovely meditation of the third stanza on where we come from and the forces that control us. The cloud has rained into a pond where it can watch itself in reflection being slowly effaced – there is no more fitting verb; it even contains "face" to go with "mirror" – by the wind:

She wrote her poem after reading Hughes' 'Lines to a Newborn'. Hughes generously and truthfully remarked that hers was "much superior" to his – in which a hand is compared to that of the Biblical Judith, who saves her people by cutting off the head of the enemy general, Holofernes, in his wine-sodden sleep.

Plath's ending lines are surely the last word in turning an infant's wail to poetry, likening its cries to ascending balloons.

The social whirl resumed. Plath and Hughes were invited by Valerie and T.S. Eliot to a supper that included Natasha and Stephen Spender; and, at a cocktail party given by Faber & Faber, Hughes was illustriously photographed with Auden, Spender, Eliot, and Louis MacNeice. Events continued on this note, with Plath writing poems and getting published, and a favourable review of *The Colossus* by A. Alvarez. Like many of his Cambridge friends, Hughes took up writing for the theatre to make money, and selling to the BBC.

Sylvia became pregnant again, but miscarried, and at the end of February 1961 was hospitalised for two weeks for an appendectomy. Meanwhile, with Ted bringing her one tasty meal a day, she read, wrote in her diary, enjoyed the flowers sent her, and observed hospital routine. Two strong poems in a voice of prose derived from her stay – 'In Plaster' and 'Tulips', both with seven-line stanzas, written on 18th March.

'In Plaster' was inspired by a woman with a body-cast in her ward. Here the protagonist amusingly pries into the relationship and the back and forth of who-holds-the-power between her plaster self and her body that does the speaking – differentiated by Plath through colour as "white" and "yellow" respectively. Through language relaxed rather than intense, Plath slips in and out of prose, yet still produces a poem. Largely, she states the obvious that most of us overlook in favour of what we think is expected. *Origin*ality comes from just this – seeing what is there at the *origin*. Drawn to our attention, it makes us inwardly start as we wonder how we missed it and that it can make poetry.

In 'Tulips', her white, quiet, peaceful state is invaded by the red tulips brought by Hughes when she only wanted to be left alone. The tulips are too ferocious to be left at large; she compares them to the inside of the mouth of a roaring "great African cat". To conclude, she sheds tears that to her taste like water from a land impossibly far away, like her health.

This was a hopeful stage, nevertheless. Hughes' *Lupercal* was awarded the Hawthornden Prize. For Plath – *The New Yorker* sent her a first-reading contract (she would be paid extra for submitting her poems to them first); Alfred Knopf planned to publish *The Colossus* in America; she won first prize in the Cheltenham Festival; the BBC broadcasted and recorded her readings of her poems; and during March she began writing her novel, *The Bell Jar*.

Hughes persuaded her, pregnant for the third time, to move to Devon. Near North Tawton they found a house with grounds they liked and could afford – Court Green. Borrowing the price, they sublet their flat to an attractive young couple, Assia and David Wevill, and moved at the end of August 1961.

Court Green

In the middle of continuing literary success, Sylvia gave birth to a son, Nicholas, in their frosty bedroom (40^{0}F) at Court Green in January of 1962. *The Colossus* attracted good reviews, though one complaint was her lack of closeness to the subjects of her poems. When spring came, she and Hughes harvested and sold up to one thousand daffodils from flower beds on their property. Plath rose early to begin four hours of writing before the children woke up. One of her most powerful poems, 'Elm', is dedicated to Ruth Fainlight (American poet, married to the British novelist Alan Sillitoe) because she liked it so much. Dated 19th April 1962, it says more than she could actually see – that Ted was distancing himself from her.

Speaking straight out as a survivor, the elm, which grew near their house, begins by saying that it does not bear the bottom, having been there with its roots. It continues, saying that we must love, and that love, fleeting, tortures us to death. Sometimes the tree speaks out straight, sometimes she is oblique with disconnected imagery, but agony always shows through. The sound of the wind holds the thunder of running horses, and the rocking of the blown tree is like a gallop that will go on, year after year, running the way love runs away, until you are dead.

The image of the tree in stanza six is visual enough to make a painting. "Sunsets", then "scorch" in the first two lines add to the colour red in the third. Then the tree, brought to life by a violent wind, all but explodes. This unique line with its crazed energy joins together different motions – from being shattered to the in-air whipping back, forth, and around of blunt, deadly clubs gone berserk, smashing self as well as anything within reach.

The moon, jealous because lifeless, also torments the tree, dragging it with her force-field – but the elm speculates that it may have caught her, then let her go, following an ordeal in the elm's massive branches.

Birds of prey that live there express the elm's emotions through their lives, but the elm can know nothing beyond longing for a love that passes away. In closing, it presents the moon as a snake-haired Medusa face. (In Greek mythology, Medusa was one of the three Gorgons, who had snakes for hair and turned to stone those who looked at them. Perseus, guided by her reflection in his shield, cut off her head.)

The inconstant moon, representing loveliness and love, is also a killer. We, fated to seek romance and love, cannot help looking at her, whereupon her rays, like Medusa's hair, impart a poison that keeps us in thrall to love. The "isolate" (meaning solitary; also unalloyed) and incessant habit of longing is a fault that destroys us.

This poem of sustained feeling is one of Plath's most painfully sad.

The Bell Jar

Busy as ever that spring, besides producing and selling more poems, Plath finished *The Bell Jar*, written in six weeks. To write it she had applied for a Saxton grant, which she was notified of winning in November of 1961. Typically organised, she had the manuscript already packaged in four lots, one to be sent before each of four payments. By then Heinemann had accepted it for publication under the pseudonym of Victoria Lucas to disguise the identifiable characters. Plath later defended their unkind portrayals by saying: "I've tried to picture my world and the people in it as seen through the distorting lens of a bell jar."

J.D. Salinger's *The Catcher in the Rye* had been a strong influence. His novel shook up the literary world in 1951 with its non-conforming prep-school male protagonist's verbal sniping at Establishment Phonies. In a similar vein, *The Bell Jar*'s deadpan humour churns and detonates continually below the narrative. With her poet's and painter's eye – a child's eye – Plath brightly animated what she saw. Her humour edged even her colour sense:

> The color scheme of the whole sanatorium seemed to be based on liver. Dark, glowering woodwork, burnt-brown leather chairs … a mottled brown linoleum …

Here, a metaphor bursts open new dimensions:

> Doctor Gordon's face lighted with a slow, almost tropical smile.

This next paragraph displays the tactility of a simple 3-D drawing or painting in words, with "copper" and "tiger-colored" adding touches of red:

> An old metal floor lamp surfaced in my mind. One of the few relics of my father's study, it was surmounted by a copper bell which held the light bulb, and from which a frayed, tiger-colored cord ran down the length of the metal stand to a socket in the wall.

And we come across passages of enchanting poetry:

> I thought the most beautiful thing in the world must be shadow, the million moving shapes and cul-de-sacs of shadow. There was shadow in bureau drawers and closets and suitcases, and shadow under houses and trees and

> stones, and shadow at the back of people's eyes and smiles, and shadow, miles and miles and miles of it, on the night side of the earth.

An image at the heart of the book is electroshock, beginning with news of the Rosenbergs' electrocution in the first sentence. Julius and Ethel Rosenberg had been found guilty of passing secret information about the atomic bomb to the Soviets in the era when Senator McCarthy was investigating espionage. The Plath-character, who would suffer bungled electroshock treatment, is horrified by the thought of electrocution, "like being burned alive along all your nerves". Beginning with her full schedule in Manhattan as a guest editor at *Mademoiselle*, the story of her breakdown leads through the first shock treatments, whose memory would always hang over her when she entered a depression. By the end she had acquired a sense of strength: "I took a deep breath and listened to the old brag of my heart. I am, I am, I am." Then, finishing the novel, she crosses a literal and figurative threshold.

The Visit

In May 1962, Assia and David Wevill, who were subletting the Hughes' flat, came down from London for the weekend. Now on her third husband, Assia, a glamorous woman who collected men and preferred poets, arrived ready to move in on Hughes, and left with a note from him saying that he wanted to see her in London. After the weekend, on 21st May, Plath wrote 'The Rabbit Catcher', a metaphor framing her rage and misery. Besides having to deal with the death of her marriage, she was afflicted by knowing that the shortened version of *The Colossus*, published in America by Knopf, had hardly been noticed.

'The Rabbit Catcher', one of her most concentrated poems, is as harrowing and violent as 'Elm', and more direct. The imagery in the opening lines make the reader realise how the violence she had prized in Hughes was turned against her. She focuses on the trapper's cruelty, never far from his lovemaking, shown by his hands that liked to kill wrapped around a tea mug as if it were a neck. Her poetic self knew more than her person could face.

On 9th July, Sylvia, who had just been saying to her visiting mother (unconvincingly) how happy she was and how perfect her life, received proof to the contrary. She answered a ringing phone before Ted could reach it, and the caller, a woman, asked for Ted in a voice she tried to disguise as a man's. Sylvia recognised Assia Wevill. From then on she knew that her marriage was over. One of her first acts of rage was to burn the new novel she was writing that was to have been for Hughes, celebrating their life-giving marriage. Soon afterwards, she burned all of Hughes' papers and manuscripts within reach as well, and her mother's hundreds of letters.

Ironically, she now began to write some of her most interesting poems since 'Elm', but almost no one wanted publish them. Alvarez, an exception, recognised how good they were.

5

The Poems

> I am not worried that poems reach relatively few people. As it is, they go surprisingly far – among strangers, around the world, even. Farther than the words of a classroom, teacher or the prescriptions of a doctor; if they are very lucky, farther than a lifetime.

If we could weigh raw poetic power on scales, Sylvia Plath's would measure in a heavyweight class. This power doesn't always resolve into poems that are perfect or even good wholes – not for Plath or any other poet. It turns up unpredictably and, after what may take long stretches of effort, finishes in the best form that the poet could effect. In Plath's case, she set up regular hours each day to coax out raw material and shape it. If some poems ask the indulgence granted the early dead, others overwhelm us with originality and life. She had a gift for hands-on imaging. When she wrote, it was as though her robust physicality kept bursting up through the underground of her psyche into highly tactile metaphors – word-objects we can relate to, so that even the most horrifying compel while they repel.

Plath's poems have brought about an equally strong critical response. While her supporters have greatly outweighed her detractors, negative comments may be instructive.

Martin Seymour-Smith, on record for showing sympathy towards women writers, in his *Guide to Modern World Literature* referred to *Ariel* as a book of minor poems. He pointed out that their subject matter reaches only as far as Plath's depressed self – her pathology – and does not extend into a reality we all can share, whose truths touch on the human condition. Her poems, despite many being well-crafted, would need to present experiences of a more universal nature to qualify as major.

He goes on to say, " … But fashionable criticism has been wrong in emphasising 'the contemporary predicament' in her poems. They should read the French essayist Simone Weil to find this: she really writes about the contemporary predicament. Sylvia Plath was writing about herself. The comparison is a revealing one …"

Her poems, like her stories, are ultimately personal. Ted Hughes wrote in his introduction to 'Johnny Panic and the Bible of Dreams', "It seems probable that her real creation was her own image, so that all her writings appear like notes and jottings directing attention towards that central problem – herself." This implies narcissism, whereas, although fame was her aim, and everything she wrote more or less straight out of her life, she properly used source-material that she found within and around herself. Poems with precise dates assigned to them provide the most profound autobiography when matched to events.

In his introduction to her *Collected Poems*, Hughes was illuminating: "Her attitude to her verse was artisan-like: if she couldn't get a table out of the material, she was quite happy to get a chair, or even a toy. The end product for her was not so much a successful poem, as something that had temporarily exhausted her ingenuity". Plath would have applauded his concrete imagery, and, while his perception endorsed her view that writing was industry, she had stated, "For me, poetry is an evasion from the real job of writing prose" and " … when I do poems, it eats up the whole day in a slow lust which I can't resist." She differentiated the two: "A poem is concentrated, a closed fist" whereas a novel is "relaxed and expansive, an open hand …"

She did everything well, she wrote verse well (as distinct from poetry), her competence with verse forms showing in childhood when she made greeting cards for her family. Among later experiments she preferred the villanelle, her favourite being 'Mad Girl's Love Song', at the back of *The Bell Jar* but not in her *Collected Poems*. Although she once had felt that "I must order life in sonnets and sestinas and provide a verbal reflector for my 60-watt lighted head", her choosing free verse as an adult was not to dodge the difficulties of poetic forms, but to best express herself.

Along with the popular poems are some less known but no less effective, and besides these, random passages that delight, or shock, or both. Sylvia's glassy, brightly-smiling persona is perfectly at odds with the savagery in some of her strongest poems (no doubt one accounting for the other).

Humour infuses her poems as well as her prose. Blended with the astonishing metaphors, it characterises her so pervasively and quietly that it may be overlooked, but once noticed, it is identifiable everywhere and never far from the disgusting, the toxic, and the ferocious.

As stated by herself and her biographers, Plath had many models (as she saw it, competitors) and many influences. From her *Journals* (29th March 1958) after she'd broken through a siege of writer's block:

> Arrogant, I think I have written lines which qualify me to be The Poetess of America (as Ted will be The Poet of England and her dominions). Who rivals? Well, in history – Sappho, Elizabeth Barrett Browning, Christina Rossetti, Amy Lowell, Emily Dickinson, Edna St Vincent Millay – all dead. Now: Edith Sitwell & Marianne Moore, the ageing giantesses & poetic godmothers ... May Swenson, Isabella Gardner, [Anne Sexton belongs here too] & most close, Adrienne Cecile Rich – who will soon be eclipsed by these eight poems: I am eager, chafing, sure of my gift, wanting only to train & teach it – I'll count the magazines & money I break open by these best eight poems from now on.

(They derive from four paintings by Klee – 'Virgin in a Tree', 'Perseus', 'Battle-Scene', and 'The Ghost's Leavetaking'; two by de Chirico – 'The Disquieting Muses' and 'On the Decline of Oracles'; and two by Rousseau – 'Snakecharmer' and the sestina, 'Yadwigha, on a Red Couch, among Lilies'.)

She emphasised a debt to Virginia Woolf's diaries and novels, while writing, "I shall go better than she … I will be stronger: I will write until I begin to speak my deep self, and then have children, and speak still deeper." Playing family politics, she claimed that their daughter Frieda was named after an aunt, but Hughes told a friend that the name was in tribute to D.H. Lawrence's wife. More directly, her publishers worried that her 'Poem for a Birthday' owed overmuch to Theodore Roethke's 'The Lost Son', even fearing a charge of plagiarism. (Hers is a far superior poem.) Interesting though these facts may be, we do best to see her as trying out her talent variously at first.

According to the British poet and writer, Robert Nye, she had jotted 'On listening to Laura Riding' on one of the drafts of 'Little Fugue'. From a meeting with Hughes, Nye bears out how significant that connection was beyond her scribbled phrase. Sylvia Plath and Ted Hughes together embodied the mythology of Robert Graves' *The White Goddess* (by then a bible for poets) in the way that Riding did with Graves, she being for him the incarnation of the Great Goddess and his Muse. Graves believed that a male poet must be in thrall to the Goddess (in her guise as mortal woman) to whom he consecrates his life, and only this will make him a true poet – a life-and-death matter. The Goddess has had her representatives in all cultures down through the ages where females were empowered, sometimes as a mother figure who gives life to the earth and all beings, sometimes as a terrifying force that destroys what she creates. Hughes most likely saw himself still sanctioned by this mythology when, feeling dulled by domesticity and piqued by a six-year itch, he switched allegiance to Assia.

Individual Poems

Along with her many selves, Plath had many voices. In a sinister poem of 1957, 'The Thin People' Plath describes a famished people whose existence is likened to the grey flat actors in early cinema. She wrote in her journal that what she feared most was the death of the imagination, which can apply here. Those, who have been starved of mind, diminish everything around them.

They parch with a look or touch, their wizened multitudes making even tree-trunks in a forest go flat, and the world papery-grey just by standing there.

The poem consists of two lines per stanza, hardly ever rhymed, but usually the end words relate loosely in sound (a frequently used technique with Plath): “drawn” – “thin”; “head” – “could”; “pales” – “smiles”; “meat” – “it”. The end word of the final, single line, “bones”, hearkens back two stanzas to “browns”, which didn’t even half-rhyme with its mate, “flatten”. Plath did not let a compulsion to rhyme, or even half-rhyme, spoil her natural diction.

Going from thin to fat, ‘Sow’, (1957 also) is an instructive example of a poem whose language never really strays beyond prose. Plath’s enthusiasm for the subject matter is prodigious, and it would be fair to say that the last line conveys an impression of poetry as it sweeps us beyond the barnyard textures into the unreal world of myth, literature, and geography. However ‘Sow’ remains prose cast into the form of a poem. Should it, therefore, still be considered a poem? One can say, yes, by the end we have experienced something of a poem’s heft. One can also say, no, we haven’t really been transported further than the “Brobdingnag” body of the sow. (Brobdingnag was the country of the huge in Swift’s satire, *Gulliver’s Travels*, lending the sow a literary cast.) This poem on her size, expressed through the vocabulary of the outsized, relates to poetry the way illustration compares to art: It discusses, it describes, but it does not create.

Other people’s poems may misfire as poetry for other reasons, such as being dry, or feeble – merely ‘poetical’. Plath may not have always achieved poetry, but she was too physical a writer to be weak or dry. When not successful, she usually tended to go off-track or keep to a prose mode.

‘Snakecharmer’ classifies as a word tableau. Plath took liberties with Rousseau’s jungle painting that inspired it. His piper is a woman, a black silhouette against a river and sky with a full moon. Hers, male, pipes up a green water-world of snakes, and a wave of “flickering grass tongues” to stand upon.

Plath, a self-confessed frequenter of the thesaurus, may

well have consulted it for her numerous snaky words – "waver", "undulate", "twine", "wave", "sway", "coiling", "writhe", "pliant", and "twist". But a list from a thesaurus could never yield up the poetry of "snake-rooted bottom of his mind"; nor a line like "reedy lengths and necks and undulatings", with its unexpected juxtapositions – the stems of different lengths rising out of the water alongside snake necks, all moving with the flow of water in time to the music.

Whoever needs refreshment before or after Plath's racking later poems should enter this 'snakedom', following the piper until he unravels us back to reality. This easy, lovely, one-colour poem goes well beyond description in the theatre of Plath's imagination.

Taking colour further, 'Medallion' (1959) complex and rich, assembles a dead snake. (Plath often mentions snakes.) As one who revelled in red (vermilion being her "color tonic"), she crafted word-ornaments here that display its variety – the snake's tongue being as sharp as an arrow and coloured rose, and the 'eye' of the medallion is vermillion in colour, compared to "garnet bits" in a split rock. There are other colours too – "orange", "bronze", "ochre", and "white"; and images that bring in colours without naming them – mostly fire-words – "ignited", "flame", "burned", "fire", "smoulder", and "sunset", and then "milk-glass". "Dark bruise" doesn't quite qualify.

Plath wrote 'Mushrooms' (1959) as an exercise. For her, contrivance could alchemize into poetry. In the first stanza, by the time you reach "quietly", the long ***i***s and the *y*s have launched the silent world of the small. Undercurrents of alliteration and assonance smoothe the poem's progress through swift, two-beat lines, as sound-play brings emphasis to the words themselves: "t***o***es" – "n***o***ses", and more long ***o***s in "h***o***ld" – "l***o***am"; "sh***o***ulder" – "h***o***les"; the beginning ***a***s in "***a***cquire" – "***a***ir"; the long ***a***s in "betr***a***ys" and "the small gr***a***ins m***a***ke room" (also its ***m***s); ***an***'s in "bl***an***d-m***an***nered"; the *s*s, *f*s, ***t***s, and ***i***s in "***s***o***ft*** ***fists*** in***sist***"; the long ***ee***s in "h***ea***ving" and "l***ea***fy" and "n***ee***dles"; the beginning ***e*** in "***ea***rless" and "***e***yeless"; and the ***uh*** in "n***u***dges" – "sh***o***vers". Most of these needn't have been laboured upon by Plath, but would have just occurred because she was tuned in to words.

The metaphors, mushrooms seen as tiny gnomes with tools, turn mushroom-material into an invincible soft force that pushes beyond adjectival description. The end doesn't rely upon hyperbole like the last line in 'Sow'. Instead the last line leaves us with a frisson. Not only will mushrooms take us over, but the vanguard's insinuating foot has become palpable – soft and white and clammy.

Plath loved flowers. 'The Beekeeper's Daughter' (1959) contains some of her most sensuous lines about flowers and their greenhouse-thick fragrance. The shape of the "mouthings" in the first line repeats in "corollas", "circle", "well", "trumpet-throats", even "burrow", then "hole-mouth". ("Many-breasted hives" is their inverse.) But the magic lies in her sumptuous creation, stunning the senses all at once with the profusion of open flowers – their colours, their damp, silken textures, and perfumes; the ruby-throated hummingbirds; and the golden pollen dropping from a flowering tree upon other blossoms. A reader is all but overcome.

In 'Leaving Early' (September 1960) Plath focuses on flora, with her opening line featuring flowers (note the alliteration and assonance – ***l***s and ***ow***s). In the eighth line the protagonist hears the cut flowers drinking [short ***i***s reinforcing each other]. In the tenth line Plath's protagonist beholds, through the mini-jungles in the room, the berries in the room. Plath made the berries even more solid than we could see them. The ***o***s, especially in "tablet***o***p", "m***o***bs", and "l***oo***king" help to round the eyeballs. In a remarkable metaphor further down, she compared chrysanthemums to the head of Holofernes. (He was the general whose head was cut off by Judith, discussed after 'Morning Song'. In paintings he has long, tousled hair.)

Two months later bric-a-brac replaces plants in 'A Life'. Here an egg-shaped glass container encloses a small Victorian-ornament world of miniature people, a curlicue sea, and ornate clouds. This landscape extends somehow to a permanently floodlit place, where a woman and her shadow go round and round (likely from Plath's terrible *Bell Jar* days). And just beyond, the bounds of the controlled, stifled picture-world are invaded at ghastly last in the two ending lines, when a drowned man emerges from the sea.

To restore us after that sea-image here are two others:

The first, magical, from 'On Deck' (July 1960) featured in lines six, seven and eight, passengers at midnight can make out in the distance an ocean liner with its portholes lit up, which is compared to a double-layer wedding cake with candles.

The second, fantastical, and showing Plath's sense of humour, is from stanza three of 'Whitsun' (14th February 1961). In this brilliant personification of the ocean, she makes it an old-fashioned Chinese gentleman, "mustachioed" with seaweed and kowtowing as it laps the shore. Not really fitting in with the rest of the poem, it seems as though Plath had inserted a treasured, spare metaphor to put this second one to use.

Perhaps she did the same with the inspired simile from 'The Manor Garden'. In a truly successful and three-dimensional transformation, plump pears dangling in a tree become little Buddhas. (When they sit in meditation, Buddhas' outlines are pear-shaped.)

'Face Lift' (15th February 1961) buttressed by slang, metaphor, and her inimitable choice of words, shows more of Plath's humour. The darning egg of 'The Disquieting Muses', appropriately slipped inside a sock here, becomes at one remove a skull beneath ageing, hanging jowls.

Plath expressed her colour-consciousness in clothes, interior decorating, and no less in her writing. In fact, almost all of her poems make use of one colour at least, or black, or white. 'In Plaster' is predominantly white; 'Tulips', red and white. Beginning 'Insomniac' (May 1961), a metaphor recalls one of the now-obsolete tribulations of typewriting when copies were made by using carbon paper soon pitted with holes made by full stops – which leads to a different white in the vintage Plath, ultra-Gothic, morbid, visually electrifying, fourth line.

The first line of 'The Surgeon at 2 a.m.' (29th September 1961), where fluorescent white light is antiseptic, doesn't prepare us for the riot of horrific depictions to come, and even if this high-voltage white doesn't compete with the white in the last line of 'Insomniac', the rest of the poem compensates by means of local colours, mostly red. The surgeon speaks, likening the patient's opened-up trunk to an overripe garden, then a sunset, where the "squeaking" is the sound of rubber gloves wet with blood. Beyond the blue glow that begins the last stanza, the poem's ending lines gesture towards pseudo health and beauty through metaphor. Note the repeated ***ay*** sounds in "gr***e***y faces", the ***u*** sounds in "sh***u***ttered by dr***u***gs", and the ***f***s in "***f***ollow" and "***f***lowers".

'Wuthering Heights', from September as well, is a descriptive landscape poem chock-full of metaphors and images. Here Plath stands straight where everything else is flattened by the wind that resembles the force of destiny. To her inimitably sharp comedic eye, the sheep are described as grandmothers. The adjective "marbly", which converts the sound of ***baa***-ing – the rapid *ah-ah-ah-ah-ah-ah* – into the sight of small, round, hard marbles in a row, is worthy of a child's uninhibited metaphor-making. Night falls with a homespun simile: the strait valleys where houses light up in the evening compare to deep, dark purses at whose bottoms glitter spilt coins.

From the same month came the pastoral 'Blackberrying'. Through the burning green of the fields, Plath follows a path that zigzags through blackberry bushes to a cliff overlooking the sea. Then she reproduces the metallic sheen and stippling of the sea in pewter and silver, as well as the noise of it being hammered. Converting water to metal that is simultaneously fluid and solid, its last two lines ring in our ears.

Hughes' familiarity with the occult yielded at least one big benefit. As Plath suffered from writer's block at times, he taught her mental exercises for accessing the subconscious, which nourished her poetry. Besides, when she couldn't think of anything to write about, he often gave her a subject. The poems worked out well if her imagination allowed itself to go crazy on the graph of normalcy – peaking, or plummeting into chasms.

One of these is 'The Moon and the Yew Tree' (22nd October 1961) that opens evoking a sci-fi dreamscape of cold imagery. Near the elm, the yew tree grew in the cemetery that bordered on Court Green. Here it shoots up and looms black above our psyches, while the moon takes over from the sun. The moon in Plath's poems is anything but the moon of the Romantics. When it appears in 'Elm', each image makes it more frightful than the last. One of Plath's favourite words, "bald", certainly suits her, and 'The Moon and the Yew Tree' ends with both herself and the tree in a blue light and at their most stark.

'Mirrors', dated the next day, takes topical description into another league. The mirror is not an inert thing, but sees with precision, thinks, and speaks. Not cruel but only truthful, it meditates on the opposite wall, so long looked at now that it has become part of the mirror's 'heart'. (The plain words that described the wall, "pink, with speckles", show again how the simplest observations can suit a poem.) The mirror is also a lake, bent over by a woman to whom it reacts. No one can forget the poem's last lines that summarise a woman's life of looking at her reflection – from enjoying her beauty to being appalled by the old, sagging face with its carp mouth.

Rage, bitterness, and black humour fired up 'The Applicant' (11th October 1962) in which a girl is a thing of parts, a talking commodity trained to be whatever a man needs, more valuable at each milestone anniversary. Finally: " … Will you marry it, marry it, marry it." The question, as a mechanized statement, slams shut with a full-stop. (One wonders if Plath was in touch with the unnatural, contrived part of herself when she wrote this poem.)

The next day, she finished her popular 'Daddy', a declaration of freedom, akin to her finally allowing herself to acknowledge negative feelings about her mother. Here she is released from being just Daddy's little girl, and it made her feel whole. She reported that when she read it aloud to a friend, both of them were rolling on the floor with laughter.

The poem works into the subject of Nazism and the Holocaust. In a BBC reading, Plath said that 'Daddy' was "spoken by a girl with an Electra complex", and "that her father was also a Nazi and her mother very possibly part Jewish". (One might also ask if Plath's being German had brought up guilt in connection with the electrocution of the Jewish Rosenbergs back in 1953.) If being of German stock in a country that fought a war against Germany hadn't erupted into problems for the family, Otto's dictatorial streak had. Now was the time to exorcise what she felt about him along with her fear of Hughes, of the bully behind the violence. Nazism perfectly supplied the images.

After ten stanzas of these, she reproduces his 1930 photograph in the words of the eleventh stanza. She had tried to find her father through attempted suicide, then through marriage in which her father morphs into a husband-authority-figure. (*Mein Kampf*, 'My Struggle' – the title of Adolf Hitler's book – presented his political philosophy along with his hatred of Jews.) The model Plath made, the man in black to whom she said "I do" in the marriage ceremony, was, of course, Hughes. His affair with Assia Wevill is referred to in the lines about the telephone being torn from the wall. When, by means of the poem, she has killed off both father-figure and father, the latter with a stake driven through his heart and townspeople cavorting on his grave, there comes her satisfying grand finale:

> Daddy, daddy, you bastard, I'm through.

Parts of this ground-breaking, sixteen-stanza poem unfortunately go loose, and it is a pity that she hadn't firmed the whole into a more consistent feat of rhyme and wit, sustaining the rhythm and the rhymed ***oo***. Perhaps she left off revising through self-indulgence, or because harvests of the subconscious, then a relatively new terrain, were winnowed less by a poet who had known writer's block.

Anything could be fodder for Plath's sense of humour. In 'Cut' (24th October 1962) she gleefully addressed a kitchen accident that had left her thumb with a slice of skin hanging on at the top and red flesh showing below. Her imagination took off, presenting her thumb as a cast of characters bleeding or dressed in bloody gauze. Among these are a "pilgrim" scalped by an Indian, a "Homunculus", then, wearing the stained bandage and a "Trepanned veteran", followed by "dirty girl", with its two ***er*** sounds that strengthen each other. The two ending words of the poem pack a punch with their ***um*** sounds and the final ***p***.

'Whiteness I Remember' (9th July 1958) is a likely precursor for 'Ariel', telling how Sam, her runaway horse, galloped along the road while she barely hung on with her arms around his neck. 'Ariel' (27th October 1962) named after the horse picked out for her riding lessons while at Court Green (and he would have been named for the sprite, Ariel, from *The Tempest*) is considered important because, like 'Daddy', it expresses her new sense of release and direction. It succeeds as an idea clinched with a fiery image; but, as examples of Plath forgoing her sense of touch, many lines are denatured in the final published form, written in a private, cryptic language requiring research into earlier, more explanatory drafts, and certainly into the symbolism of Tarot card 14 for clarification. (Plath's interest in this was due to Hughes'.) 'Ariel' tells of flesh released into spirit, of the unstoppable surge into a sexual climax, and of herself speeding towards transformation as she galloped out of the world straight into the rising sun.

The end is indeed exultant. Regrettably, we are tripped up by the idea of dew flying, too unformed as a collective entity to manage propulsion, and by many prior images that have to be worked out. Still, the way a jockey's verve transmits itself to the horse and lifts him in his speed, Sylvia's rapture fuels her race full-tilt into the sunrise.

She had made two early suicide attempts – the first, trying to drown herself; the second, narrated in *The Bell Jar*. Her third death in the poem, 'Lady Lazarus', completes its meaning. Brash and one-of-a-kind like 'Daddy', it gleams with black humour, but behind this and the terrifying images, we hear, as it accumulates, a cry from the heart. In the second and third stanzas Plath again identifies with Jews in relation to Nazis. Written 23rd – 29th October of 1962, in the middle of anger and anguish, she shows an acute sense of helplessness and of inevitable death in the face of her situation. The fifteenth stanza has been widely quoted. If the next three lines with their loose rhymes poured out easily, it was because she meant what she was saying: that she tries to die in order to make it hurt and feel authentic. Too many of her recent experiences must have seemed anaesthetized or meaningless. And – black humour again – after doing it often enough, she wisecracked, "I guess you could say I've a call."

In the last four stanzas, she has turned to fire. More holocaust depictions – her fat has been melted down to make soap; and only a gold wedding ring and a tooth-filling can be found in her ashes. But she warns God and the devil of her phoenix-like return in the last two stanzas.

Although Plath may have associated her means of suicide with the murder of Jews in gas chambers, she most likely chose her way to die for practical reasons.

The weight of words thuds down in the first word – "Axes" – of 'Words', one of her four last poems, dated 1st February 1963. "Rings", the verb that describes the sound of the whacked wood, also implies the circular pattern of sound waves – the echoes – the meanings – reverberating in all directions from the word spoken (the axe in action) as if from a struck bell. Plath compares them to horses running outwards. They carry into the hearer's mind, through his reaction, and all down the chain of consequences. (Note the gallop of hoof-beats in "indefatigable", two dactyls in the second line of the last stanza.)

The words are by now without weight, merely responded to through habit, but the effects continue, following the direction of fate. In the ending's matter-of-fact and anti-sensational language, water, which began as sap flowing from the struck wood, comes to rest in one of Plath's beautiful images. Looking down at faint, submerged points of light that gleam in a pool, we are suddenly awestruck to realize that we are seeing deep into the universe where infinities of stars trap us in our destiny.

Please notice that whatever correct meaning this paraphrase may contain, it cannot do justice to the poem's fabulous mystery. Always the most economical way – and the only way – of putting something, good poetry means exactly what it says. In the same sense that there are no synonyms, there is no paraphrase.

Alone

After a failed attempt at a reconciliation with Hughes in Ireland, Plath had to face raising the children and looking after Court Green alone. She filed for a legal separation and continued writing poems, telling her mother in a letter that she was a genius of a writer and that her present poems would make her name.

When she read them to A. Alvarez in London, he was very enthusiastic, saying that the way she talked about having written them sounded to him "like demonic possession." She organised them in a collection to be named *Ariel and Other Poems*. The periodicals to which she then submitted them rejected all but a very few. Furthering her grim state, Heinemann was having problems finding a publisher for *The Bell Jar* in America. With typical pluck, however, Plath kept on writing poems and even started a new novel.

In December of 1962 she moved with Frieda and Nicholas to London. Although she had many friends, she remained lonely, and fell ill with sinusitis and then flu that the children caught. Through this worst winter in living memory, water pipes froze and her flat was often without heat or electricity. Hughes would come by to see the children, which upset her further. Still, she continued to write.

Dated the same day as 'Balloons' (hard to believe), her last poem is 'Edge'. Its first line strikes like a hammer. Always wanting to be perfect and then desiring death, Plath may have been writing about herself. The dead woman is a horizontal Greek statue. Two dead children, like white serpents with their small, smooth, white limbs, "coil" at – presumably the woman's breasts – implying the asp held by Cleopatra. (The adjectives "dead" and "white" reinforce the statue image, while "scroll" and "coil" recreate the carving.) Sylvia, who found her deepest connectedness to be motherhood, turned a symbol of tender fulfilment into one of horror, sadness, and death.

Now that her life is over, the woman has taken them back into her body, the way a rose, symbol of love, shuts when the garden that fluttered all day with convoluted shapes and colours, "stiffens" at night. Through this verb we see both an array of sturdy phallic stalks, and frost threatening blooms with rigor mortis. Just as the previous image presented mothering and death together, "stiffens" hints at both sex and death.

Night is the time when wanton night flowers open up for

business. They secrete not perfumes, but "odors", deeper than the cosmetic and the gorgeous, beneath which may arise a whiff of decay, of death again. These odors don't behave like a blend of air and mist: they "bleed" – mortality hovers nigh. (Note mutual reinforcement of meaning through the ***ee*** in "bl***ee***d", "sw***ee***t", and "d***ee***p".) The flower suggests an openness to love (with the ***o*** in "***o***dors" and "thr***o***ats") in which the carnal and the morbid are coupled.

The last four lines give us Plath's strangest, strongest moon – a half-moon – and created without even one adjective. Once long ago she might have cared, but now she has been there, seen that – and her gazing is as hollow as a skull's.

The last line, with the short ***a*** sound repeated three times to drive home the "bl***a***cks", may conjure up night in a witches' woods brittle with dead underbrush, the air alive with static electricity. One can't know that Plath didn't use "cr***a***ckle" and "dr***a***g" for the sound, letting the sense take care of itself.

Only a very sure poet could have written 'Balloons', discussed in the Prologue, and 'Edge', both being simultaneously laden and economical. These two entirely diverse poems of Tuesday, 5th February, are her last.

Five Days

Seeing Plath's condition as serious, her doctor put her on antidepressants while he tried to get her a hospital bed. On Thursday, 7th February, in a desperate state, she took the children to spend a few days with her friends Gillian and Gerry Becker. On Friday evening she went out, taking party clothes, and later, according to Hughes, spent a short time with him. When she returned, the Beckers noticed her changed – energized. On Sunday, although pressed to stay, she asked to be driven home. The neighbour in the flat below reported hearing her footsteps all night until about 5.00 a.m. on Monday morning. Within a few hours she was found, with the doors taped and her head still in the oven, dead from gas poisoning. She had left bread and milk for the children in their room, and on her desk the manuscript *Ariel and Other Poems*.

Epilogue

The two journals that cover the final three years of Sylvia Plath's life are missing – the first has vanished; the second, written in as late as her last three days, was destroyed by Hughes, his reason being that this was for their children's sake.

When he said, cryptically, after Plath's death, "It was her or me", he may have meant that he feared death as a poet if he failed to follow the imperative of *The White Goddess*, a charge he never stinted. Assia, ever eclipsed by Plath's posthumous dazzle, committed suicide in 1969, also using gas, with Shura, her four-year-old daughter by Ted Hughes, beside her. Hughes married Carol Orchard the year after.

As custodian of Sylvia Plath's estate, he proceeded to publish her work in discrete selections, thus maximizing profits, for she had become a cult figure. In 1982 *The Collected Poems* won the Pulitzer prize.

Summing Up

As the new slips away into the old, there are questions about Plath's work staying in print in an ever-growing canon of literature, and her poems earning space in anthologies. The answer is that a combination of talent, daring, and drama guarantees her poems an aura, even if not always a cult status, that will keep them onstage for a long time, with her prose in the wings ready to share a spotlight.

The Unabridged Journals, where Plath practised her craft, will always stand tall without the poems, and remain a model for young would-be writers to see what it takes to succeed. It is also a record of time and place as lived in by an ambitious girl. *The Bell Jar*, entertaining autobiography at least, and the uneven collection of short stories, are the result of the practice that went into the *Journals*, illustrating stages in Plath's career as well as aspects of herself. Even her *Letters* to some extent may be considered literary productions. With this variety of works available, interested readers can see how the prose relates to the poetry.

Beyond rules, and always in an immediate present, Plath's poems will continue to excite both the young and the youthful, even after her romance and suicide become footnotes. Those, who are creative, are remembered by masterpieces and forgiven for lesser productions. Their awkward, obscure, or low-voltage works may, however, enclose unexpected treasures.

An example of a poem by Plath that hardly communicates anything at all is 'The Couriers' (4th November 1962) said to be less obscure in draft form, but in *The Collected Poems* stays locked within occult references. Yet it contains an intriguing mythic image, of a talking cauldron.

To choose her best we might ask: How deeply does a particular poem matter to us? Does it stick to the point or wander off, blunting its thrust? How original and plentiful are the images?

Poems of great charm and unbroken energy that are widely read include 'Mushrooms', 'Snakecharmer', and the poems for, and about, her children. Sensational with its wild brilliance, 'The Surgeon at 2 a.m.', is well known, too, although like 'Wuthering Heights' and 'Blackberrying' it remains primarily descriptive (though of a far different order than the prosaic 'Sow', also appreciated). We can relate to Plath's strangeness – never a deliberate, postcard exotic – because of her tactile, even visceral renditions. For instance, at the start of 'Burning the Letters', those thrown-out pieces of paper crumpled up into white balls are seen as "fists" – both for the shape and for the impact of their words. Towards the end of 'Mystic', she turns the sun concretely into a cardinal-red "geranium". And a piece of seaweed suggests pubic hair in the last line of 'Berck-Plage'. In being familiar, everything is possible in her torrent of connectedness through metaphors and similes.

For the purposes of a hypothetical future anthology, however, we must also look for emotional weight.

Instead of containing images, 'The Applicant' embodies one. Funny and bitter in its depiction of how society designates a wife, it represents Plath's most concentrated anger. The poem is consistent within itself, except that the black suit in the middle fits oddly.

'Mirror', quirky, mattering widely to men as well as women, and somewhere between description and something deeper, is one of her best and best liked. Its imagery stays on track, swerving only very slightly when the mirror is compared to the "eye" of a rectangular deity, and we scramble to visualise such a god.

In the formidable 'Elm' (a wych elm), the third line of the fifth stanza halts the flow while we puzzle out the meaning. Specifically, the wych elm's rough leaves and downy twigs can catch enough rain for it to appear light grey, appropriate enough for poison. We can assume that no matter how far-fetched, all of Plath's images had a reasonable basis somewhere. The strong ending also requires scrutiny, offered earlier in this *Guide*. When completely clear to the reader, 'Elm' should then be reread without interruption. It ranks at the top with 'The Rabbit Catcher', where the image of hands, ringing the mug, removes us from the landscape to a kitchen only for a split second. For its naked, agonized, overwhelming, and sustained intensity, this poem of pure force may be considered her best. Speaking for many, 'Elm' and 'The Rabbit Catcher' fill a need and will continue to do so for as long as people give everything in love.

In 1984, Ted Hughes became the Poet Laureate. He died in October of 1998. His last words were from a poem of his, 'The Offers' (published 10 days before in *Howls and Whispers*) in which Sylvia appeared to him from the dead, saying "This time, don't fail me." Literary personage, poet, and playwright, he will be especially remembered for one poem, 'The Thought Fox', written in 1957, out of a collection that runs well over a thousand pages.

Although nothing is clear about what happened when Sylvia went out on the evening of 8th February 1963, we know that she saw Ted, and possibly learned that Assia was pregnant.

In her journal she had written, 3rd January 1959, "All my life

I have been 'stood up' emotionally by the people I loved most: Daddy dying and leaving me, mother somehow not there." The loss of Hughes came on top of an already shaky foundation. She must have been aware that another breakdown was possible, requiring shock treatments again and leading to loss of custody of the children.

Balancing that, though, her children and professional success were still there to enjoy, and she had made plans for the near future. During the hopeless days of no light, heat, or water, the Beckers had invited her to stay on, although she insisted on going home that evening against their kind urgings and her doctor's warnings to them not to leave her alone.

Her hosts had reported that when she returned on 8th February, she seemed enlivened by a purpose. We cannot necessarily interpret this as a plan for suicide. At that moment she may have been just as easily inspired to move forward.

A depressed poet may commit suicide to secure fame, revenge, or relief. (Fame – so intensely coveted by her friend, the poet Anne Sexton, that she who had planned suicide for herself later, was angry at being upstaged!) Maybe an irresistible idea had been hurled into the thick of Sylvia's depression: the only way she would be loved was to be dead. Sylvia had written to her mother, saying that Ted had wished her dead a number of times. That in itself could not have been enough for her to take her own life, but combined with depression and the new medication, could have effected a warped seeing as if through the glass of the bell jar. The terror of another breakdown with its consequences had become a palpable enemy, and the idea of suicide a familiar friend. She had written, "How did I know that someday – at college, in Europe, somewhere, anywhere – the bell jar, with its stifling distortions, wouldn't descend again?" Against this she knew she was helpless.

Whatever the reason, her suicide made sure that her presence would blaze beside Ted Hughes for the rest of his life.

Selected Bibliography

By Sylvia Plath

The Collected Poems, introduced and edited by Ted Hughes (HarperPerennial, 1992). Contains important contributions by Hughes, especially the list and ordering of poems that Plath intended for *Ariel*. The three indices need revising.

The Unabridged Journals of Sylvia Plath (Random House, 2000). Their availability long overdue, these present the rich strata of Plath's perceptions.

Letters Home, edited, and with introduction and commentaries by Aurelia Schober Plath (Harper & Row, 1975). A good companion to the *Journals*. Many photographs.

The Bell Jar (Harper & Row, 1971). Plath's favourite villanelle, 'Mad Girl's Love Song', omitted from *The Collected Poems*, may be found at the end of this bestselling autobiographical novel.

Johnny Panic and the Bible of Dreams, Introduction by Ted Hughes (HarperCollins, 1977). To be read for the Introduction and biographical aspects, as well as the text.

About Sylvia Plath

Paul Alexander, *Rough Magic* (Da Capo Press, 1999). Exhaustively informative and admirably fleshed out with detail. Starts with Plath's grandparents and ends with a visit to her grave in 1988. Contains a section of photographs of Plath from age two through to 1959 with Hughes, and includes some of her friends.

Jillian Becker, *Giving Up: The Last Days of Sylvia Plath* (St. Martin's Press, 2003). A short memoir on Plath's last difficult days and tormented nights.

Ted Hughes, *Birthday Letters* (1998) and *Howls and Whispers* (1998) from *Collected Poems* (Faber & Faber, 2003). A poet's power of description brings Plath to life in glimpses.
Diane Middlebrook, *Her Husband: Hughes and Plath – A Marriage* (Viking, 2003). Expands from biography to develop ideas and information about both Plath and Hughes, and Hughes' later life. Important reading, along with Plath's biography. Random photographs – of Hughes and his brother in 1947, of Plath, her children, and others including Assia Wevill, and Hughes in 1986.
Linda Wagner-Martin, *Sylvia Plath, A Literary Life* (Palgrave MacMillan, 2003). A useful, succinct survey of Plath's poems and prose, as well as of her life.
Richard Wilbur, 'Cottage Street, 1953'. One of his most moving poems.

Note

A search on the Internet for Sylvia Plath (through *Google*) demonstrates her popularity better than anything else, particularly the *Sylvia Plath Forum.*

GREENWICH EXCHANGE BOOKS

STUDENT GUIDE LITERARY SERIES

The Greenwich Exchange Student Guide Literary Series is a collection of critical essays of major or contemporary serious writers in English and selected European languages. The series is for the student, the teacher and 'common readers' and is an ideal resource for libraries. The *Times Educational Supplement* praised these books, saying, "The style of [this series] has a pressure of meaning behind it. Readers should learn from that … If art is about selection, perception and taste, then this is it."

(ISBN prefix 1-871551- applies)
All books are paperbacks unless otherwise stated

The series includes:
W.H. Auden by Stephen Wade (36-6)
Honoré de Balzac by Wendy Mercer (48-X)
William Blake by Peter Davies (27-7)
The Brontës by Peter Davies (24-2)
Robert Browning by John Lucas (59-5)
Lord Byron by Andrew Keanie (83-9)
Samuel Taylor Coleridge by Andrew Keanie (64-1)
Joseph Conrad by Martin Seymour-Smith (18-8)
William Cowper by Michael Thorn (25-0)
Charles Dickens by Robert Giddings (26-9)
Emily Dickinson by Marnie Pomeroy (68-4)
John Donne by Sean Haldane (23-4)
Ford Madox Ford by Anthony Fowles (63-3)
The Stagecraft of Brian Friel by David Grant (74-9)
Robert Frost by Warren Hope (70-6)
Thomas Hardy by Sean Haldane (33-1)
Seamus Heaney by Warren Hope (37-4)
Joseph Heller by Anthony Fowles (84-6)
Gerard Manley Hopkins by Sean Sheehan (77-3)
James Joyce by Michael Murphy (73-0)
Laughter in the Dark – The Plays of Joe Orton by Arthur Burke (56-0)
Philip Larkin by Warren Hope (35-8)
Sylvia Plath by Marnie Pomeroy (88-9)
Poets of the First World War by John Greening (79-X)

Philip Roth by Paul McDonald (72-2)
Shakespeare's *A Midsummer Night's Dream* by Matt Simpson (90-0)
Shakespeare's *King Lear* by Peter Davies (95-1)
Shakespeare's *Macbeth* by Matt Simpson (69-2)
Shakespeare's *Othello* by Matt Simpson (71-4)
Shakespeare's *The Tempest* by Matt Simpson (75-7)
Shakespeare's *Twelfth Night* by Matt Simpson (86-2)
Shakespeare's *The Winter's Tale* by John Lucas (80-3)
Shakespeare's Non-Dramatic Poetry by Martin Seymour-Smith (22-6)
Shakespeare's Sonnets by Martin Seymour-Smith (38-2)
Tobias Smollett by Robert Giddings (21-8)
Dylan Thomas by Peter Davies (78-1)
Alfred, Lord Tennyson by Michael Thorn (20-X)
William Wordsworth by Andrew Keanie (57-9)
W.B. Yeats by John Greening (34-X)

LITERATURE & BIOGRAPHY

Matthew Arnold and 'Thyrsis' *by Patrick Carill Connolly*
Matthew Arnold (1822-1888) was a leading poet, intellect and aesthete of the Victorian epoch. He is now best known for his strictures as a literary and cultural critic, and educationist. After a long period of neglect, his views have come in for a re-evaluation. Arnold's poetry remains less well known, yet his poems and his understanding of poetry, which defied the conventions of his time, were central to his achievement.
The author traces Arnold's intellectual and poetic development, showing how his poetry gathers its meanings from a lifetime's study of European literature and philosophy. Connolly's unique exegesis of 'Thyrsis' draws upon a wide-ranging analysis of the pastoral and its associated myths in both classical and native cultures. This study shows lucidly and in detail how Arnold encouraged the intense reflection of the mind on the subject placed before it, believing in " ... the all importance of the choice of the subject, the necessity of accurate observation; and subordinate character of expression."
Patrick Carill Connolly gained his English degree at Reading University and taught English literature abroad for a number of years before returning to Britain. He is now a civil servant living in London.
2004 • 180 pages • ISBN 1-871551-61-7

The Author, the Book and the Reader *by Robert Giddings*
This collection of essays analyses the effects of changing technology and the attendant commercial pressures on literary styles and subject matter. Authors covered include Charles Dickens, Tobias Smollett, Mark Twain, Dr Johnson and John le Carré.
1991 • 220 pages • illustrated • ISBN 1-871551-01-3

Body of Truth: D.H. Lawrence: The Nomadic Years, 1919-1930
by Philip Callow
Philip Callow's outstanding account of D.H. Lawrence's last years provides a fresh insight into Lawrence's art as well as his life. Candid about the relationship between Lawrence and his wife, it shows nevertheless the strength of the bond between them. Lawrence's constant quest for renewal through sexual energy is shown against the backdrop of his failing health. If no other book has persuaded the reader of Lawrence's greatness, this one does.
Philip Callow – biographer, novelist and poet – has also written lives of Chekhov, Cézanne, Robert Louis Stevenson, Walt Whitman, and Van Gogh, all published to critical acclaim. His biography of D.H. Lawrence's early years, *Son and Lover,* was widely praised.
2006 • 290 pages • ISBN 1-871551-82-X

Aleister Crowley and the Cult of Pan *by Paul Newman*
Few more nightmarish figures stalk English literature than Aleister Crowley (1875-1947), poet, magician, mountaineer and agent provocateur. In this groundbreaking study, Paul Newman dives into the occult mire of Crowley's works and fishes out gems and grotesqueries that are by turns ethereal, sublime, pornographic and horrifying. Like Oscar Wilde before him, Crowley stood in "symbolic relationship to his age" and to contemporaries like Rupert Brooke, G.K. Chesterton and the Portuguese modernist, Fernando Pessoa. An influential exponent of the cult of the Great God Pan, his essentially 'pagan' outlook was shared by major European writers as well as English novelists like E.M. Forster, D.H. Lawrence and Arthur Machen.
Paul Newman lives in Cornwall. Editor of the literary magazine *Abraxas*, he has written over ten books.
2004 • 222 pages • ISBN 1-871551-66-8

John Dryden *by Anthony Fowles*
Of all the poets of the Augustan age, John Dryden was the most worldly. Anthony Fowles traces Dryden's evolution from 'wordsmith' to major

poet.

This critical study shows a poet of vigour and technical panache whose art was forged in the heat and battle of a turbulent polemical and pamphleteering age. Although Dryden's status as a literary critic has long been established, Fowles draws attention to his neglected achievements as a translator of poetry. He deals also with the less well-known aspects of Dryden's work – his plays and occasional pieces.

Born in London and educated at the Universities of Oxford and Southern California, Anthony Fowles began his career in film-making before becoming an author of film and television scripts and more than twenty books. Readers will welcome the many contemporary references to novels and film with which Fowles illuminates the life and work of this decisively influential English poetic voice.

2003 • 292 pages • ISBN 1-871551-58-7

The Good That We Do *by John Lucas*

John Lucas' book blends fiction, biography and social history in order to tell the story of his grandfather, Horace Kelly. Headteacher of a succession of elementary schools in impoverished areas of London, 'Hod' Kelly was also a keen cricketer, a devotee of the music hall, and included among his friends the great trade union leader Ernest Bevin. In telling the story of his life, Lucas has provided a fascinating range of insights into the lives of ordinary Londoners from the First World War until the outbreak of the Second World War. Threaded throughout is an account of such people's hunger for education, and of the different ways government, church and educational officialdom ministered to that hunger. *The Good That We Do* is both a study of one man and of a period when England changed, drastically and forever.

John Lucas is Professor Emeritus of the Universities of Loughborough and Nottingham Trent. He is the author of numerous works of a critical and scholarly nature and has published seven collections of poetry.

2001 • 214 pages • ISBN 1-871551-54-4

In Pursuit of Lewis Carroll *by Raphael Shaberman*

Sherlock Holmes and the author uncover new evidence in their investigations into the mysterious life and writing of Lewis Carroll. They examine published works by Carroll that have been overlooked by previous commentators. A newly-discovered poem, almost certainly by Carroll, is published here.

Amongst many aspects of Carroll's highly complex personality, this book explores his relationship with his parents, numerous child friends,

and the formidable Mrs Liddell, mother of the immortal Alice. Raphael Shaberman was a founder member of the Lewis Carroll Society and a teacher of autistic children.
1994 • 118 pages • illustrated • ISBN 1-871551-13-7

Liar! Liar!: Jack Kerouac – Novelist *by R.J. Ellis*
The fullest study of Jack Kerouac's fiction to date. It is the first book to devote an individual chapter to every one of his novels. *On the Road*, *Visions of Cody* and *The Subterraneans* are reread in-depth, in a new and exciting way. *Visions of Gerard* and *Doctor Sax* are also strikingly reinterpreted, as are other daringly innovative writings, like 'The Railroad Earth' and his "try at a spontaneous *Finnegans Wake*" – *Old Angel Midnight*. Neglected writings, such as *Tristessa* and *Big Sur*, are also analysed, alongside better-known novels such as *Dharma Bums* and *Desolation Angels*.
R.J. Ellis is Senior Lecturer in English at Nottingham Trent University.
1999 • 294 pages • ISBN 1-871551-53-6

Musical Offering *by Yolanthe Leigh*
In a series of vivid sketches, anecdotes and reflections, Yolanthe Leigh tells the story of her growing up in the Poland of the 1930s and the Second World War. These are poignant episodes of a child's first encounters with both the enchantments and the cruelties of the world; and from a later time, stark memories of the brutality of the Nazi invasion, and the hardships of student life in Warsaw under the Occupation. But most of all this is a record of inward development; passages of remarkable intensity and simplicity describe the girl's response to religion, to music, and to her discovery of philosophy.
Yolanthe Leigh was formerly a Lecturer in Philosophy at Reading University.
2000 • 56 pages • ISBN: 1-871551-46-3

Norman Cameron *by Warren Hope*
Norman Cameron's poetry was admired by W.H. Auden, celebrated by Dylan Thomas and valued by Robert Graves. He was described by Martin Seymour-Smith as, "one of ... the most rewarding and pure poets of his generation ..." and is at last given a full-length biography. This eminently sociable man, who had periods of darkness and despair, wrote little poetry by comparison with others of his time, but it is always of a consistently high quality – imaginative and profound.
2000 • 220 pages • illustrated • ISBN 1-871551-05-6

POETRY

Adam's Thoughts in Winter *by Warren Hope*
Warren Hope's poems have appeared from time to time in a number of literary periodicals, pamphlets and anthologies on both sides of the Atlantic. They appeal to lovers of poetry everywhere. His poems are brief, clear, frequently lyrical, characterised by wit, but often distinguished by tenderness. The poems gathered in this first book-length collection counter the brutalising ethos of contemporary life, speaking of, and for, the virtues of modesty, honesty and gentleness in an individual, memorable way.
2000 • 46 pages • ISBN 1-871551-40-4

Baudelaire: Les Fleurs du Mal *Translated by F.W. Leakey*
Selected poems from *Les Fleurs du Mal* are translated with parallel French texts and are designed to be read with pleasure by readers who have no French as well as those who are practised in the French language. F.W. Leakey was Professor of French in the University of London. As a scholar, critic and teacher he specialised in the work of Baudelaire for 50 years and published a number of books on the poet.
2001 • 152 pages • ISBN 1-871551-10-2

'The Last Blackbird' and other poems by Ralph Hodgson *edited and introduced by John Harding*
Ralph Hodgson (1871-1962) was a poet and illustrator whose most influential and enduring work appeared to great acclaim just prior to, and during, the First World War. His work is imbued with a spiritual passion for the beauty of creation and the mystery of existence. This new selection brings together, for the first time in 40 years, some of the most beautiful and powerful 'hymns to life' in the English language. John Harding lives in London. He is a freelance writer and teacher and is Ralph Hodgson's biographer.
2004 • 70 pages • ISBN 1-871551-81-1

Lines from the Stone Age *by Sean Haldane*
Reviewing Sean Haldane's 1992 volume *Desire in Belfast*, Robert Nye wrote in *The Times* that "Haldane can be sure of his place among the English poets." This place is not yet a conspicuous one, mainly because his early volumes appeared in Canada, and because he has earned his living by other means than literature. Despite this, his poems have always had their circle of readers. The 60 previously unpublished poems of

Lines from the Stone Age – "lines of longing, terror, pride, lust and pain" – may widen this circle.
2000 • 52 pages • ISBN 1-871551-39-0

Martin Seymour-Smith – Collected Poems *edited by Peter Davies*
To the general public Martin Seymour-Smith (1928-1998) is known as a distinguished literary biographer, notably of Robert Graves, Rudyard Kipling and Thomas Hardy. To such figures as John Dover Wilson, William Empson, Stephen Spender and Anthony Burgess, he was regarded as one of the most independently-minded scholars of his generation, through his pioneering critical edition of Shakespeare's *Sonnets*, and his magisterial *Guide to Modern World Literature.*
To his fellow poets, Graves, James Reeves, C.H. Sisson and Robert Nye – he was first and foremost a poet. As this collection demonstrates, at the centre of the poems is a passionate engagement with Man, his sexuality and his personal relationships.
2006 • 182 pages • ISBN 1-871551-47-1

Shakespeare's Sonnets *by Martin Seymour-Smith*
Martin Seymour-Smith's outstanding achievement lies in the field of literary biography and criticism. In 1963 he produced his comprehensive edition, in the old spelling, of *Shakespeare's Sonnets* (here revised and corrected by himself and Peter Davies in 1998). With its landmark introduction and its brilliant critical commentary on each sonnet, it was praised by William Empson and John Dover Wilson. Stephen Spender said of him "I greatly admire Martin Seymour-Smith for the independence of his views and the great interest of his mind"; and both Robert Graves and Anthony Burgess described him as the leading critic of his time. His exegesis of the *Sonnets* remains unsurpassed.
2001 • 194 pages • ISBN 1-871551-38-2

The Rain and the Glass *by Robert Nye*
When Robert Nye's first poems were published, G.S. Fraser declared in the *Times Literary Supplement*: "Here is a proper poet, though it is hard to see how the larger literary public (greedy for flattery of their own concerns) could be brought to recognize that. But other proper poets – how many of them are left? – will recognize one of themselves." Since then Nye has become known to a large public for his novels, especially *Falstaff* (1976), winner of the Hawthornden Prize and The Guardian Fiction Prize, and *The Late Mr Shakespeare* (1998). But his true vocation has always been poetry, and it is as a poet that he is best

known to his fellow poets. "Nye is the inheritor of a poetic tradition that runs from Donne and Ralegh to Edward Thomas and Robert Graves," wrote James Aitchison in 1990, while the critic Gabriel Josipovici has described him as "one of the most interesting poets writing today, with a voice unlike that of any of his contemporaries".

This book contains all the poems Nye has written since his *Collected Poems* of 1995, together with his own selection from that volume. An introduction, telling the story of his poetic beginnings, affirms Nye's unfashionable belief in inspiration, as well as defining that quality of unforced truth which distinguishes the best of his work: "I have spent my life trying to write poems, but the poems gathered here came mostly when I was not."

2005 • 132 pages • ISBN 1-871551-41-2

Wilderness *by Martin Seymour-Smith*

This is Martin Seymour-Smith's first publication of his poetry for more than twenty years. This collection of 36 poems is a fearless account of an inner life of love, frustration, guilt, laughter and the celebration of others. He is best known to the general public as the author of the controversial and bestselling *Hardy* (1994).

1994 • 52 pages • ISBN 1-871551-08-0

BUSINESS

English Language Skills *by Vera Hughes*

If you want to be sure, (as a student, or in your business or personal life), that your written English is correct, this book is for you. Vera Hughes' aim is to help you to remember the basic rules of spelling, grammar and punctuation. 'Noun', 'verb', 'subject', 'object' and 'adjective' are the only technical terms used. The book teaches the clear, accurate English required by the business and office world. It coaches acceptable current usage and makes the rules easier to remember.

Vera Hughes was a civil servant and is a trainer and author of training manuals.

2002 • 142 pages • ISBN 1-871551-60-9

The Essential Accounting Dictionary of Key Financial Terms

by Linda Hodgson

This is a key aide for students seeking examination success in Accounting A-Level and GNVQ Advanced Business. It results from work with teachers and students and addresses common difficulties. Straight-forward, easy to read definitions of key financial terms – which form the basis of understanding and better performance at tests and examination. There is a multiple choice quiz to crosscheck how much the student knows.

Linda Jane Hodgson, graduate in History and Politics, is a former Tax Inspector and qualified teacher. Professionally, she also advised accounting firms on taxation. She now teaches business and finance at a London college.

1999 • 150 pages • ISBN 1-871551-50-1